Pulled from the Ashes

JULIE CHEREPANOV LEWIN
WITH R. CHARLES SHIPMAN

Pulled from the Ashes

ISBN 978-0-9779692-8-9

Table of Contents

Acknowledgments

Julie wishes to thank:
Dr. Roger W. Popp, thank you for believing in me.
You are the best chiropractor in the world.
Thank you for your nutrition advice.

Carl, you are closer to me than a brother, and you are always
watching out for me. Thank you for all your help,
with editing and more. You've taught me a lot.

Gary, thank you for being a good husband and friend.
You have given me all the room I needed to grow.

Katie and Melissa, you are the best daughters a mother
could ever ask for. You are both grown now and
you've never given me a minute of grief.
May God bless you both.

Ж

Carl thanks:
Merry, being the sweetest of wives, for putting up with me.

Ж

Randy Conger, thank you for being who you are.

God, thank You for creating me and
for the parents you gave me.

Flight

Anya could fight the tears no longer. *This has been our happy home*, she thought. Ever since the day when she and Alixey fell in love, she had known they would raise their family and grow old here. *Now where are we going? We know no one there and everyone here.* Memory after memory went through her mind. *I grew up around these people. My childhood friends are now my neighbors, and my daughters are friends with their children.* She sat up and wept quietly as the wagon rolled on.

Suddenly a small whimper broke the silence. It was Anuta. "What is wrong, little one?" Anya asked through her own tears while Alixey was busy guiding the horses.

"I want Murka and Kiska to come too," she answered.

"Cats don't like to travel, my little one. They don't like to ride in wagons. Besides they are going to keep Uncle Petro, Uncle Daved, and Grandmama company."

Anuta quieted down but was not satisfied.

As they approached the river, they heard the sound of the running water. The full moon, reflecting on the water, helped them see their way. "Everyone hold on!" Alixey instructed, almost shouting. He slowed the horses.

As the wagon rolled into the water, the sound got louder.

The horses protested but Alixey snapped the reins again. "Come on, come on!" he commanded quietly. They began to obey and started across. The rocky bottom of the river caused the wagon to sway and jerk even more, creaking as it slowly moved forward.

The thought of the wagon turning over on its side plagued Anya. Her heart pounded. She gripped the seat on either side of her lap. Alixey snapped the reins and gave the horses commands again and again. The girls just doggedly hung on.

Finally they were coming up onto the opposite bank of the river. Not sure if they had attracted attention, Alixey snapped the reins and commanded the horses to climb up the steep bank. Each foot they got closer to China was one foot further from their loved ones. Sadness and emptiness washed over Alixey and Anya. They were leaving behind their mother, father, and siblings, but they had no choice; they had to go.

Anya

1
Nikolayevska

Alixey and Anya had laughed and played together as children. Anya was stronger than Alixey and pinned him when they wrestled. She gave him piggyback rides across the river. They had grown up together. When they fell in love, they knew that they would marry and live happily ever after in this idyllic little village of Nikolayevska in a beautiful valley in the Altai Mountains with the majestic Ob River running through it.

The village was a tightly knit community, quiet, ideal for raising a family. Everyone was happy there. All the families were friends. The homes were built by their own hard labor. Their children played in the woods across the river on the hills just outside the village. They planted their wheat and gardens in a common area, and there were never disagreements about it. There was a sawmill, a grain mill and plenty of livestock. They all had their own fenced-in areas for their cattle. The horses were hobbled and let out to graze in nearby fields. There was a midwife for childbirth and an herbalist if one became ill. If a family fell on hard times, everyone would get together and gather enough provisions to get them through. They practiced "love thy neighbor" every day.

The hills teemed with wild game. The river, spanned by a bridge consisting of three logs tied together with a railing on one side, supplied all their outside needs; it was shallow in spots where a wagon could be driven across, but nothing was across the river but dense woods.

Early in the morning, smoke would start to rise from the chimneys all through the village. After breakfast everyone would go about their daily duties. Alixey owned the grain mill; every day he would hurry out to it, where someone would be waiting to have his grain milled. Anya stayed home with their two daughters, five-year-old Anuta and three-year-old Tanya. The barnyard was full of chickens, ducks, and geese and all needed tending. Anya would throw grain out for them in the mornings and collect their eggs in the evening. The cows needed to be milked both morning and evening. There was fresh milk and eggs every day. The wheat, the potatoes and the gardens were growing and needed to be weeded. There were plenty of fish to be caught in the river.

The bees were about their business every day, flying from flower to flower and filling the beehives with honey. Once a year, the families of the village harvested the honey, took it to town and traded it for gold. They had pooled their gold to buy the valley and build this village, which now consisted of about one hundred people, to maintain their religious beliefs and escape the atheism that was pervading the country.

All seemed perfect, except for the fear and heaviness that hung like an invisible fog over the village. Stalin, the communist leader of Russia, had been taking over all the land and evicting the land owners. It was a new order. Everyone had to surrender all possessions, which now belonged to all the people. Trying not to dwell on it too deeply, the villagers went about their daily duties, wondering what would become of them. They hoped their idyllic little village would be forgotten since it was so deep in the mountains. Some hoped that life would go on as usual; others prayed.

One quiet summer evening, Alixey and his lovely family were eating dinner. The girls were talking about how they each caught a chicken, wrapped them up like babies and played with them as the chickens protested, then finally escaped.

Suddenly a loud knock at the door startled everyone. Alixey wondered who would be coming over at this late hour but walked slowly over and opened the door. On the other side stood a soldier. By the buttons and emblems of his uniform Alixey knew he was one of Stalin's goons. With cold black eyes, he identified himself and unemotionally gave Alixey and his family an eviction notice. They were to leave the home that he had built with the help of his family and friends and move into the chicken coop. Their house would be turned into a school. Alixey's topaz blue eyes were bloodshot from the anger that surged through him. A weight fell on him as the soldier informed him he had thirty days to complete this task. His strong muscular body felt weak, his legs felt like rubber, his hands shook and his lips quivered.

The soldier started to leave but turned back to him. "Oh, one more thing," he said. "If anyone tries to flee, he will be shot, gladly. We will be patrolling the road and watching this whole village." Without another word, he turned and walked over to his horse, mounted and spurred it. He violently jerked the reins to the right, almost causing the horse to stumble, and rode off.

"Who was that?" Anya asked. She had not heard any of the conversation but only that it was the voice of another man.

"An agent of the devil," Alixey answered, surprising his wife.

She hurried over as he tried to read the paper that he had been given, but the light in the room was too dim; he could not make out what was written on it. She could see how angry her husband was; she knew this was a serious situation. She asked him again, "What did he say, Alixey?"

"They are evicting us from our house. We have thirty days to move into the chicken coop." His answer was laced with anger.

Anya was an emotionally strong woman, but this news went through her like lightning on a stormy night. Filled with the same rage and anger as her husband, she gave him an answer that surprised him. "Well, let them have it, if they want it so bad. We are NOT defeated. We still have one another. We are survivors; let them have it. We cannot fight the whole system; we need to stay alive for our children." Taking him by the arm and tugging him toward the dining room, she added, "Let's finish our supper."

Anuta was sitting at the table. She knew something was wrong but quietly ate.

Tanya was being a three-year-old; she sat at the table swinging her legs and humming something to herself.

Alixey remembered his widowed mother and two younger brothers; surely they would have already gotten the news since they lived closer to the entrance of the village. "Anya, I have to go. Mama and my brothers probably have received the news. When I leave, bolt the door and do not open it for anyone." He stepped out the door, closed it, heard the bolt come down and quickly set off in the direction of his mother's house. He felt himself slumping from the thoughts that bombarded him. He had promised his dying father he would take care of his mother and brothers.

Anger rushed at him like a sudden blast of wind, and he began punching the air. "I bought the land! I cut the trees! I built that house!" His voice pierced the quiet surroundings. "I prepared every log. Not Soviet Russia, not Stalin. I did!"

Before he knew it, he was at his mother's door. "Mama, it's Alixey," he called out as he knocked. "Let me in!"

His brother Petro was standing just inside. He was pale; the blood had drained from his face. Alixey could see that they had received the news. Petro motioned him in. As Alixey stepped into the house, he could see his mother sitting at the table. She appeared scared and bewildered. As soon as she saw Alixey, she stood up. Alixey walked over to her, reached out, grabbed her and pulled her into his arms and tried to comfort her, but she was inconsolable.

"Mama, God will see us through this. Don't worry, Mama, everything will be okay." Alixey remembered Anya's words. "We are not defeated, Mama."

Mama's voice was angry and loud. "The man told us to move into the chicken coop. They need this house as their command post. They gave us thirty days. Your father built this house, not Stalin or his new order. Your father!" she shouted. Overcome with grief, she sat back down, her face soaked with tears.

"Mama, God will see us through this. He knows what we should do. Mama, now I need to go home to my girls. I will check on you in the morning. Now, when I leave, bolt the door and don't let anyone in."

Heading home in the dark, Alixey met up with Vasili, his neighbor, on his way to see his sister and her family. They tried to comfort one another at first, but both knew it was time for planning: what to do, how to proceed.

"We are not going to give our lives over to these people," Vasili told Alixey. "Masha and I have received the news that we are to surrender our livestock. Well, they can have it. We are fleeing to China; there is no Stalin there. We are young enough to start over. Come with us," Vasili urged him.

7

Alixey sighed and hesitated for a moment. "I will talk to Anya," he replied. Wishing each other well, they went their own ways.

Alixey, now standing in front of his door, gently knocked. "Anya, open the door," he quietly called out. He heard footsteps, then the door was unbolted and opened. He could see his wife had been crying.

"Where are the girls?" he asked.

"Upstairs in bed."

Alixey took her hand and led her to the dining room, pointed to a chair and motioned her to sit. Anya sat down, and Alixey sat in the chair next to her trying to find the words so as not to bring more grief upon his wilted wife. "You know I love you and the girls very, very much. You are my life." He spoke quietly. "You are the reason I work so hard each day. But now things have changed—life has changed. We can comply and be puppets or we can..." His voice cracked and he fell silent for a moment. "Or we lcan flee to China. There is no communism there. We can start over again like you said."

Anya, a reasonable woman, was silent for a moment, and then asked, "When do we leave, and what if we are caught?"

"No, Anya, we will not be caught. God will help us like He always has. We can load only what we must have, make it look like we are loading grain to take to the mill. Mama and my brothers will meet us here. We will head toward the mill, but this time we just keep going. It is our mill. What questions will be asked?"

Anya held her face in her hands for a moment, and then asked, "Have you talked to your mama, Petro or Daved?"

"Not yet. I will go over there in the morning."

Just then he heard a little voice asking from the top of the stairs, "Can I go too?" It was little Tanya.

8

"I want to go too!" called out Anuta.

"No, honey. You will go with me to see Grandmama and Grandpapa," her mother informed her.

In a moment they were both at the bottom of the stairs. Alixey looked at his very blond blue-eyed girls. They could pass for twins, except for the two years difference. Anuta was a little bit bossy, though somewhat shy, but constantly analyzed everything and spoke her mind. Tanya was fearless and did not inherit one drop of shyness. She could talk to anyone anywhere, so she had to be watched all the time.

Anya, having two brothers and three sisters, was the youngest of six children. Her parents, Feodor and Fedosia, lived outside the village on a large reindeer ranch where they made a good living harvesting honey and reindeer horns. The horns were in high demand. The tips were dried and ground up for medicinal purposes while the main part of the horns was sawn into medallions for buttons.

As Anya and Anuta walked into her parents' house, she sensed a looming dark cloud of heaviness rather than her mother's usual cheeriness. The smell of freshly baked bread did not help at all.

"Mama, Papa!" Anya called out.

They called back to her from the family room, and she went in to see them sitting with her brother Simon. Everyone looked burdened and afraid, exactly the way her heart felt and her face reflected. Her father invited her to sit in a chair that he had built from saplings. Wasting no time, she began to explain why she was there.

"My dearest family," she started. "Alixey and I have decided to leave this country. We are going to China, and I think all of you should come along."

9

"No, my darling," her father replied. "We are too old to start over. You are young; go with our blessing."

Anya never argued with her parents. She had been raised to respect her parents and her elders. In her heart she knew they would not go, but she must at least try to talk them into it.

Simon could not go either. He had to stay and take care of them. His wife Nadiya would not leave her own family behind. She used to be a happy woman, but of late she seemed distant to Simon and it broke his heart. Theirs was an arranged marriage, but Simon had been in love with Nadiya beforehand.

Simon was a tall, well-built, dark and handsome man. He had his mother's dark hair, eyes and round face. He also had her demeanor and compassion, but for some reason his wife seemed to have fallen out of love with him and had become cold. He hoped she would start to love him again, so he constantly tried to earn it from her.

Nor would Anya's brother Oseph and his wife Zenya go if her parents did not. They lived in another village, and it would take up too much time to go visit them, so she didn't even try. This was too bad, as neither of her brothers had children, and it would make the trip easier to have them along.

Her three sisters had married and were living in other surrounding villages. There was no time to contact them. Feodor and Fedosia each hugged their granddaughter and tearfully wished her and her family a safe trip.

Anya took Anuta's hand and headed for the door. She turned back to take one more look at her parents, her brothers and their wives. She might never see them again. "Mama, Papa, Simon, Oseph. I don't know what day we are leaving, but I will try to send word as soon as we get settled." Without another word she and Anuta left. She was hoping they would change their minds. She never dreamed she would have to say this type

10

of goodbye to them. Walking away, she could not let herself get too emotional; she had to focus on preparing for the long dangerous journey.

While walking home Anya had to explain to Anuta that she needed her help to prepare for a long trip.

"What trip, mama?"

"A long, far away trip," her mother answered.

Out of respect for her visibly stressed mother, Anuta did not ask any more questions. She trusted her parents implicitly. She would find out soon enough.

Alixey and Anya spent a difficult night; both feared their unknown future. But reason seemed to soothe them; after all, there was no future here. Both of the girls were spirited and would not thrive in this suffocating darkness.

Morning found Anya in the kitchen with two batches of bread dough already rising, breakfast cooking on the stove, and all her clay jars of honey sitting on the floor by the door ready to be carried to the wagon. Alixey loved the delicious breakfast smells. It brought him brief comfort until he remembered the task awaiting him. He went over to Anya, gave her a hug and told her he was going to go talk to his mother and then to Vasili.

Tanya appeared from around the corner with her shoes on the wrong feet. "I'm ready to go, Papa." Her voice was crisp and clear. Alixey noticed her shoes and chuckled to himself at her sweet young innocence. He took her by the hand, and they both went out the door. Alixey closed it behind them and set out for his mother's. Hanging onto Tanya's small hand brought him comfort. Joy found a momentary place in his heart.

As Alixey approached his mother's home, he could hear strange voices and loud cries from his mother. Her voice kept crying, "Why are you doing this? Why are you taking my livestock?"

There was silence for a moment; then a man's voice said, "These are our chickens."

He heard a lot of commotion from the chickens. Alixey was not sure it had been a good idea to bring Tanya, but he quickened his pace. As he entered the yard, he could see Daved trying to comfort his mother as the horses were being led out of the barnyard by uniformed soldiers. The chickens had scattered, and two soldiers gave up the chase. Alixey stood in silence until the soldiers left. He then quietly motioned for Daved to take Mama into the house and followed, still holding Tanya's hand.

After the door was closed behind them, he asked them to sit down around the table, and then he looked around and through the window to be sure no one was listening. The anger subsiding, he asked if the two remaining horses were theirs to keep.

Petro nodded silently.

"How about the wagon?" Alixey asked.

"It's also ours," spoke up Mama, her voice laced with anger.

"And the sleigh?" asked Alixey again.

"I suppose it too is ours," answered Mama.

Alixey took a deep breath and then let out a sigh. Making eye contact with each of them, he spoke slowly and quietly. "I want you to listen to me very carefully. Anya and I have decided to flee to China. We have nothing left here."

Tanya sat on his lap. She understood that something was wrong and remained silent as the adults continued to speak.

"Where in China?" asked Mama, her voice still filled with tension.

"Urumqi," answered Alixey. "They do not turn away illegal aliens, and it is not difficult to obtain permanent residency. Once we are established there we can move elsewhere if we need to."

2
Plans

Alixey continued, "Now, Mama, we leave in three days. Petro, Daved, make sure the wagon is ready for the trip. Check the horses' shoes and hooves. Mama, bake bread, then dry it so it does not mold on the trip. Boil eggs, potatoes, bring salted pork bellies and honey. We can use the honey to trade for possessions. Pack only what you must have. Bring all the blankets and warm clothes. Then in three days, pack the wagon like you are taking grain to the mill. My family and I will meet up with you and just keep going. If anything happens and things do not turn out as planned, stay here and cooperate. I will find a way to come back for you. I promise I will get you out."

All three silently nodded their heads in agreement. "Now," spoke up Alixey again, "I need to go see Vasili. He is fleeing before we do, so you know we will all be watched very closely." With that, Alixey lifted Tanya off his lap, and he stood up as the rest remained seated. A thought came to him. "That morning, light a fire in your stove, so when the patrol comes through, they will see the smoke rising from your chimney, and they will have nothing to suspect." Everyone once again nodded as his mother wept quietly. She was so afraid of what might happen. If anything went wrong, they could be executed or imprisoned. Alixey walked over to her and kissed her cheek, then took Tanya's left hand and walked out the door. Petro followed, closed the door behind him and watched him leave.

Alixey was almost to Vasili's house when he noticed there was no smoke rising from the chimney. "Oh, he must have left during the night," he said to himself. Fearful thoughts flooded his mind. He swept Tanya into his arms and ran toward the house, seeing no sign of anyone, the barn and chicken coop open, chickens running everywhere, a cow grazing in the front yard.

Alixey went to the door and knocked. No one answered. He pushed it open, but no one was inside. Everything was a mess. It seemed they had packed up in the night and fled. He went to the barn. Wagon and horses were gone. "They fled," he said under his breath. He was sad and glad at the same time. "They had no children and needed no time to prepare."

He went home and told his wife the news. "So, it has started," she said. "All of us will now be watched closer."

The three days dragged on slowly as the many needed preparations were made. The wagon was checked for cracks; the wheels were examined and the axles greased.

Alixey checked the hooves of his two most worn-out horses—somehow knowing the soldiers would come and collect his younger and stronger ones—to ensure the shoes were properly attached and rubbed down their backs around the bridle. So when they showed up the next morning and, as expected, left him the two oldest he was not surprised but was grateful that God had given him that warning. As he stood watching the soldiers lead his horses away, including some that he had owned from birth, his heart ached. He felt sick to his stomach. But he had to keep a lid on his emotions; he had a lot to do.

Anuta came over and stood beside him. In a weak voice she asked, "Papa, are they also going to take Murka and Kiska?"

"No, my little one," he answered with a sigh. "They only take horses and cows, not cats." He took Anuta by the shoulder and led her into the house.

"We need to start loading the wagon," he said to Anya. He picked up a sack and started for the door.

Suddenly he heard a male voice say, "No! Not now. Wait!" Not knowing where this voice came from or who said it, he stood frozen, looking around. Only his wife and daughters were in the house. He set the bag down.

"Did you hear that?" he asked Anya.

"Hear what?" she asked with a very puzzled look. "What did you hear?" she asked again. Now she was confused.

"I heard a man's voice say, 'No! Not now. Wait!'" he exclaimed, "when I picked up this sack to take to the wagon," pointing to the sack beside him on the floor.

"Well, then you'd better listen," Anya said.

Suddenly there was a commotion in the village. They could hear gunshots and loud strange voices coming from the direction of Vasili and Masha's house. "Oh, no," he thought, "the soldiers have discovered Vasili's empty house." The shots were to alert other soldiers.

Sure enough, soon soldiers flooded the area. Alixey was deeply worried and thought, *How will we accomplish this task?* So he prayed, "Oh, God of heaven and earth, please help us escape this dark prison. Please keep us all safe and protect us from their watchful eyes."

Then a still small voice spoke to him. "Take courage. Wait until dusk, and then put the canopy on the wagon while it is in the barn. Load up after dusk. Your mother is being watched; they suspect her. When you go, leave her here for now; you can come

15

back for her another time. You must leave tonight. Cross the river in the shallows. Don't go near the grain mill. Your wagon will make it across without any problems. I will be there for you," the welcome voice instructed him.

All his life he had been told that God was to be feared because He always saw all our sins. He was a God who punished those who sinned against Him. Alixey did not know what he had done to win God's grace, but he was grateful.

Alixey had grown up along the river and knew all its geography. He knew exactly where the ford was.

"Anya," Alixey said excitedly. "God just spoke to me again. He told me what to do and which direction to go in." He hesitated for a moment, then continued, "We have to leave Mama, Daved and Petro behind." His voice had become sad and quiet.

Anya could see the sadness in his face. Her heart, too, was aching, and she hated the thought of leaving her own family. She drew in a breath then through a sigh said, "God doesn't speak to people. He is holy and we are not."

Alixey fixed his eyes on the floor. "Yes, He is holy, Anya, but I heard Him. He did speak to me, and I would be a fool not to listen," Alixey answered, remembering his boyhood days when he would go out to the forest and find a comfortable spot where he would sit and talk to God as if He were a friend. This was something he had never revealed to anyone before.

Alixey looked up at his wife and continued, "He said we are to wait until dark to leave." Then he nodded his head as if responding to someone. "I have to go and talk to Mama and my brothers. I will be back as soon as I can." He walked over to Anya and gave her a kiss on the cheek. He knew she also was in great turmoil about leaving her family behind.

He started toward the door, and Tanya came toward him to go along. He heard her footsteps, turned and picked her up, and carried her to her mother. "Little one," he said, "this time I have to go alone, but I will be back soon." He quickly turned and left.

Quietly he approached his mother's house. Three mounted soldiers, the same ones who had been patrolling the roads and all around the houses, seemed to be observing the house. They did not see him at first, so he shuffled his feet to make noise.

Finally they saw him; one pointed his rifle at him and demanded he state his business.

Alixey lifted his hands where they could see them and quickly said, "I 'm here to check on my widowed mother and brothers."

Satisfied with his answer, the soldier lowered his rifle. In the same threatening voice, he asked Alixey, "Do you know the whereabouts of the family that live in the house next to yours? They are gone, and we demand to know where they are."

"No, I did not know they were gone," Alixey answered, acting surprised. The soldier's glare was fixed on Alixey as he continued to speak. "Well, you let your people know that anyone caught running will be shot." He emphasized the "will."

Alixey was shaking inside. His heart in his throat, he nodded as anger pulsated through his whole body. He felt he had enough strength to take on all three of these men. He told himself over and over to act calm and control himself. If he spoke, his words would flow through his anger and give him away.

At length common sense prevailed and he turned, went to the door and gently knocked. "Mama, it's Alixey," he called out quietly. After a few moments Petro opened the door. Everyone inside seemed shaken up. A fire was going in the stove and bags were packed, sitting in the corner to his right. "Mama, Petro, Daved," Alixey stuttered, then found the words he needed. "The soldiers suspect something. I just had an encounter with them."

Petro interrupted. "They were in the barn looking at our wagon a little while ago. We were about to start loading when they showed up."

Alixey was feeling very uneasy and blinking as if he had been hit with a gust of wind. Finally he spoke up again. "Mama, Petro, Daved, my family and I are going to run tonight, and I know you are being watched, so stay here and cooperate. Start cleaning the chicken coop; make it into a house to ward off all suspicion. As soon as I get my family settled, I will come back for you. I promise." He wanted to say more but sadness overcame him, and his voice began trembling from the burden that weighed so heavily on him.

They quickly gathered around him while his mama sobbed and Petro and Daved wished him well and expressed their hope for his safe trip. Seeing his mother trembling, he reached out and took her in his arms.

Her voice shook as she asked, "Son, will I ever see you again?"

Alixey kissed her cheek and reassured her. "Mama, I will be back for you, I promise. Don't be afraid; be strong, Mama." After instructing Petro and Daved to take care of their mother and themselves, he hugged each of them, turned and left.

At home, Anya had breakfast on the table. He was too upset to eat, but for the girls' sake he sat with them, not saying a word. Apprehension and terror were their uninvited guests.

Dusk fell. Soon it would be time to pack and leave. Alixey thanked Anya for the lovely dinner and told her he would do the dishes. After piling them into the large dishpan, he went to the river to wash them while Anya dressed the girls and packed their bedding, and then he went to the barn, where he put the canopy on the wagon and hitched the two horses to it. Even though there was a full moon that night, he was confident God would blanket them with His protection from the soldiers that could surround them at any moment. Together they carried their belongings to the wagon and packed them in tightly, leaving a spot for the girls to sit in the front near them. Everything was loaded and ready to go.

Alixey went to the house, took both girls by the hand, and hurried them to the barn, where he lifted each of them in turn up onto the wagon. After Anya opened the chicken coop door and let the cow out of the corral, Alixey helped her up into the wagon and then walked around to the other side and climbed up himself. He looked around to see if everyone was seated, took a deep breath and let it out. "Hold on, here we go!" He snapped the reins, the horses jerked and the wagon started to roll as Alixey guided the horses toward the river.

3

The Journey

As they crossed the river, Alixey and Anya comforted the children about leaving the cats behind, but they had a more difficult time comforting themselves as they thought of all that they were leaving behind in their cozy little hamlet.

Once they made a good distance from Nikolayevska, they stopped to rest the horses and bedded down for the night. Anya and Anuta spread a blanket underneath the wagon and arranged the pillows. The girls fell asleep quickly, but Alixey and Anya spent a very restless night.

In the morning, Anya sliced up some bread and peeled eggs. Alixey checked the horses and led them to the nearby stream to water them. He washed up and filled a few jugs with water. When the horses were again hitched to the wagon, they all ate a quick breakfast, climbed back on the wagon and were once more on their way.

Anuta, tired of the silence, wanted a story. She thought for a moment then begged, "Papa, tell me and Tanya how you met and married Mama."

He looked over at his beloved wife with her beautiful dark shiny hair, welcoming brown eyes and round face. After a short silence, he smiled at the memories and began.

"Well," he said, "when I was seventeen years old, I was on my way home from fishing on the upper Ob River. It was a lovely sunny day. The birds were chirping, and there was a gentle sweet breeze. Every time the breeze stirred the air, it carried the lovely smell of the wildflowers.

"Well, as I walked along, I thought I heard a young lady's voice calling, 'Stop! Stop!' then I heard the bushes crackle and rocks rumbling. Once more that voice called, 'Stop! Stop!' Well, I knew she needed help. Suddenly, a reindeer ran right out in front of me with a rope tied to one of its antlers. Your mama was hanging on to the other end of the rope, and the reindeer was dragging her. I dropped my fish and my fishing pole and ran out ahead of the reindeer. I jumped out in front of it waving my arms and yelled, 'Stop now!'

"Now, a reindeer can be very mean, but this poor reindeer was so startled, it lost its footing and fell to its knees instead. I quickly went over to your mother. One look and I lost my heart. It was love at first sight. I suddenly found the strength of ten men, grabbed the rope from her hands and took control of the startled animal.

"She was all scraped up. Her hair had twigs in it, and it was sticking out everywhere. Her dress was torn in several places and had grass stains from being dragged through the field. As I was helping her up, your uncles Simon and Oseph showed up. Apparently, the reindeer escaped, and your mother tried to lasso him. She only got him by the antlers and away they went.

"She was a spirited young lady. I knew who she was, and I knew her family, but I had never really paid much attention to her before. But now I was in love.

"On Sunday when all of the teenagers went out to the woods to play, I always stayed close to her so we could talk and plan our future. I kept it a secret to protect her from gossip.

"My parents had mentioned several times that when I turned nineteen they would choose a wife for me. So one cold winter morning just after my nineteenth birthday, right after I was done leading the cows and horses to the river for a drink, they sprang the news on me. They had chosen a bride! That night we were all going to her house, and I was going to propose to her. I told them I didn't even like her, but they didn't want to hear any of that. They were friends with her parents and wanted to become related.

"I poured my heart out to them about how much I loved your mother, but they said, 'She is too spirited. You will never be able to control her.'

"I didn't want a woman to control; I wanted someone to love and that would love me, but they wouldn't listen. They said, 'Go clean up and dress nice, then hitch the horses to the sleigh.'

"Well, we were all taught to honor our parents. I went and cleaned up and dressed like they told me and went out to the barn to hitch the horses. But the main reason I went out to the barn was to pray. Well, you can imagine how hard I prayed while I was hitching the horses!

"I was expecting something earthshaking, but instead God sent me a manure pile, and I stepped in it. Feeling helpless, I kept hitching the horses to the sleigh. The smell of manure started to bug me. Then a thought hit me: *How in the world would this stuff smell in my armpits?* I shook my head. I couldn't believe I was thinking such a devious thing. But all of a sudden I thought, *Yeah, it is a good idea. What woman would agree to marry a smelly man?* I thought about it for a minute. 'Yeah, this will work,' I said, right out loud."

Both girls were laughing as Alixey continued.

"So I unbuttoned my coat, untied my sash, scooped up some cow manure and smeared it in my armpits. I wiped my hands, tied my sash back on, buttoned my coat, finished hitching the horses to the sleigh, brought them to the front of the house and went in to get my parents. My mama was in the kitchen peeling garlic to put into a slow simmering pot of soup. *Garlic*, I thought, *I wonder if she will like garlic breath.* I walked into the kitchen to tell Mama the sleigh was ready. She dropped the already chopped garlic into the soup pot and took off her apron.

"'I will go and get your papa.' she said, 'and we will leave. So go to the sleigh.'

"When she left, I took a garlic clove, peeled it and placed it between my cheek and back teeth. Like a good boy, I went and sat in the back seat of the sleigh. Well, word travels fast in a small village. I was sure your mama had heard about the other girl. I wanted to protect her from all this, but for now I was stuck. I was praying that girl's nose was working really well that night. We pulled up in front of her house, and my mama and papa went in first. They were so excited! I walked in behind them, praying, and saw the young lady working at her sewing machine. Her father asked her to come join us, and her papa brought out a chair for her and another one for me. I quietly sat next to her, still praying really hard.

"She knew right away what this was all about. After all, this was the way it was typically done. My papa looked at me and asked, 'Well, what did we come for?'

"Traditionally the groom takes off his coat to show off his strong well-dressed body. By this time I was starting to smell, so I took off my coat, stood right next to her, maneuvered the garlic between my back teeth and bit down. I got down on one knee, took her hand in mine and asked her the question I was saving for your mother. 'Would you be my bride?'

"She looked horrified! She looked at her mama and papa, and then back at me. She jumped to her feet and blurted out, 'You must be joking!' and ran out of the room yelling something I didn't understand. *Thank you, cow manure and garlic, and thank you God. Now perhaps my parents will let me marry the one I love!*

"Her papa followed her. 'Sweetheart, are you sure? Think about it,' I heard him ask.

"'No, I will not marry him!' she yelled back.

"*Oh, thank you, God,* I thought to myself. I was afraid my parents would discover my plot, so I put my coat back on and excused myself, acting disappointed, and went outside right away so they wouldn't smell me. Later that night, I explained to my parents how much I loved Mama, but they wouldn't answer. After everyone was asleep, I cleaned myself up, snuck out and ran to your mama's house. After I threw several snowballs, she finally came to the window.

"It took me a while to get her to come out and talk. As I explained everything to her, she started crying. She thought I had thrown her aside for the other girl. I reassured her that our parents would let us get married eventually. She could smell the garlic and the manure. She said I'd better not ever smell like that again!

"A week later, my mama and papa and I went to your mama's house. They said yes, and so did Mama."

Alixey reached out and took Anya's hand in his and gently and lovingly squeezed it. "We will be just fine, Anya," he assured her.

She loved this man. She would follow him anywhere in the world. She relaxed and felt cheerier.

Every so often the travelers stopped to let the horses graze and rest and get a drink of water.

After several days of travel, the hills seemed softer and were covered with tall green grass that swayed in the breeze as if to a melody. "We are in China," said Alixey, sighing with relief. They were all worn out from worry. Soldiers might have caught them; the result would have been death in front of a firing squad. Bears could have come after them, and during the night venomous snakes were about. Instead it was over; they had reached their destination. Now they needed to find a place to call home.

4
China

The girls looked around at all the gentle hills. Having lived in a valley surrounded by tall mountains, they had not seen hills like these.

The family kept traveling until they saw children playing and something that looked like a barn. But where was the house? As they drew closer, they finally saw it, dug into a large hill. It puzzled them because the whole region had sections of dense forest. There were plenty of trees for building large homes, enough to build a whole village.

None of the travelers spoke Chinese, only Russian and the language of the nomads, who were Muslims, so they just called it the Muslim language. (Probably it was Bashkir.)

As they rode up, the local children ran inside the house. Soon a man came out who was not Chinese. He was a nomad. The nomads frequently came to the Russian villages to buy honey and grain. When they showed up, they would stay for days to rest up from the long trip. Alixey and Anya and their children spoke the nomad's language. That was how they knew to run to China; they had heard about it for years. These nomads traveled from China to Russia so much that they had created a road. All Alixey had had to do was to follow it.

Alixey stopped the wagon, and the man approached them. They greeted one another and introduced themselves. The man said his name was Meernu. Alixey told him of his flight and of the oppression that was taking over in Russia.

Meernu invited them to stay with him and his family, but Alixey informed him that they were interested in buying something as soon as possible. Meernu knew of a place further south that included lots of land, but there were no close neighbors. Alixey and Anya took a minute to talk it over and decided to go see.

Meernu disappeared into the barn and came out moments later leading a horse by the reins. This horse had no saddle. Meernu effortlessly hopped on and gave him a gentle kick. The horse did not seem to mind, and off they went, with Alixey following closely.

Truly this was a beautiful area, with lots of timber, tall grass and a river perfect for fishing and all their other needs. They would be safe here. The children could grow up unthreatened by war or famine.

They finally reached a home also dug into the ground very much like Meernu's. At least it would be a shelter to keep them safe, and once they obtained their permanent residency, they could build an above-ground home.

They climbed down from the wagon and went into the empty but interesting dwelling. Two small windows on either side of the front door gave the only light; lanterns would have to be kept burning to light the rest of the house. A bread oven and a cook stove, opposite a dining table, were the only furnishings in the kitchen. Walls and ceiling of rough boards kept the dirt from falling into the two small bedrooms and family room. The dirt floors were so well packed they were perfectly smooth.

The barn, with a large corral in the back, was big enough for several cows. The river was very close, just on the other side of the road that ran past the large front yard. They would not have a very long walk to fetch water or wash dishes; they could hear the whisper of the water from the kitchen. This was a perfect place, with lots of room to spread out. The hills were full of wildflowers, ideal for bees.

Meernu was very welcoming and friendly; his big brown eyes and weathered face showed a lot of his teeth when he smiled. His black hair and olive skin made his teeth look whiter than they really were.

Alixey and Anya decided right away they would buy it. Meernu had been put in charge of selling this serene property when an elderly couple that could not work it any longer moved further south to be near their children. Alixey shook Meernu's hand and arranged to sign the papers in town the next day.

First, they needed to unload the wagon and hobble their horses to be released to graze and rest. The horses had accomplished a great feat for being so old.

Once the wagon was unloaded, Anya and the girls went inside to set up the kitchen. Alixey took a saw to cut young trees for bed frames.

Alixey and Anya worked hard; their hearts were on the family they had left behind in agreement that once all was done and they were settled, Alixey would go get them.

The barn was falling apart. It took time, but Alixey completed all the repairs to it. He went to buy hay, grain and chickens and sectioned off a portion of the barn for them. He bought one cow that the previous owner had been milking. He built four beehives on a hill where there were a lot of wildflowers and berry vines and hoped that a swarm of bees would fly by and that they might be able to catch it.

One afternoon Anya was at the river scrubbing her husband's clothes in a large metal tub using an old washboard. The board buzzed as she ran his pants up and down. She lifted the pants up to see if she had succeeded in taking out the stains around the knees, but, holding them up, she was still hearing the buzz. Puzzled, she straightened up and dropped the pants back in the tub to see what could be making such a sound. As it grew louder, she realized a swarm of bees was coming her way. They must have outgrown their hives, split up and started looking for a new home. She needed to attract them by making noise—loudly!—and finding something dark for them to land on. Hollering for her husband and children, she dumped the clothes out of the washtub, grabbed it and ran toward the house. "Bees! Alixey, there is a swarm of bees coming this way!"

Alixey, now hearing them also, came out of the barn with Anuta and Tanya right behind him. "Anuta, go in the house and get the blanket from our bed and bring it here, quickly!" he said. He was so excited. Finally they would have their bees, if they could only attract them. Anya was banging on the bottom of the tub and calling out to them. Picking up a stick, Alixey also started banging on the tub. *This is splendid*, he thought.

Anuta disappeared into the house and reappeared with a dark blanket, which they stretched out on the grass in their front yard. All of them were making as much noise as possible, yelling, screaming and banging on the washtub.

Moments later, they could see the swarm coming at them like a small black cloud. One by one the bees, still buzzing, lit on the blanket. After the bees were settled, Alixey and his family gently folded the blanket on itself once, then one more time. They also folded the long ends of the blanket so no bees could escape.

Carefully they picked it up and carried it to the hives. Alixey took the lids off and shook some of the bees into each hive.

Anya turned to Anuta and asked her and her sister to go get four empty bowls and a jug of honey.

"Why do we need honey, Mama?" Anuta asked.

"The bees are hungry. We need to feed them so they will know this is their new home," her mother replied.

Anuta and Tanya were excited over the bees. Anuta turned and ran through the tall grass toward the house with Tanya following. The grass was up to Tanya's waist. She loved the swishing sound it made as she ran through it.

When the girls returned with the honey and bowls, Alixey carefully placed a bowl in each hive. He had worked around bees all his life and had no fear of them. He replaced the lids and told his family he needed to go for a walk.

He turned and walked over the hill to the other side where he wouldn't be seen. Sitting down, he quietly started to thank God for sending the swarm. Now they could count on harvesting honey the following year. They would have enough for themselves and some to sell. He would be making a long journey on foot to Russia—a horse would be spotted and and he could be arrested or even shot. The trip would be hard, he knew, and his wife would worry. She did not know anyone here well enough to have formed any friendships. She would be responsible for caring for the girls and animals all on her own. He asked God for His mercy and strength and protection. Fall was approaching, and he would be leaving after it froze; it would not thaw again until spring. The bears would be hibernating and so would the snakes. The freezing cold weather would be torture, but he had no choice. He would miss his family here as much as he missed his family in Nikolayevska. As he sat there, he poured out his heart out to God, asking Him to take his worry and grateful for His goodness.

5

Return

Winter was now in full force. The snow was over a foot deep, and the wind was whistling. Now Alixey understood why the homes were the way they were. There was no draft except what came in when the door was opened. They stayed very warm and less wood needed to be burned. That was one less worry that he would have while he was gone.

Knowing how hard the trip would be on Alixey, Anya kept a cheerful appearance as she packed; it would be one less worry for him. Several loaves of freshly baked bread cut into cubes and then dried. A jug of honey—for energy—into which he could dip the bread cubes. Lots of venison jerky. A small pot so he could boil snow, drop in the jerky, and drink something hot before settling down somewhere for the night. She stuffed a large bearskin blanket—a very warm one—into his knapsack.

Alixey oiled his rifle and made sure that he had plenty of ammunition. The bears were hibernating, but the wolves were vicious and especially hungry this time of year. The cold and the search for food drove them down to the lower elevations. He hoped he would not run into any. His rifle held a single shot, and

31

they ran in packs. With God's help they would not detect him. Perhaps the long bearskin coat would disguise his scent.

He dressed as warmly as he could. He put on the thick shirt and pants that his wife had made him a few years before. Next, a wool sweater, two pairs of wool socks, his boots, the full length bearskin coat, his furry rabbit skin hat, and finally a wool scarf. He wrapped the scarf around his neck and over his nose and mouth. He had to be careful not to burn his lungs with the frigid air.

Anya helped Alixey with the pack. As he kissed and hugged her, she clung to him, not wanting to release him. But at last she kissed him and let him go. He had to leave, and she and the girls must wait at home.

Alixey kissed the girls and instructed them to behave. He hated to leave them, but his mother and brothers needed him to make the terrible trip. "Family does for family" was what he had been told since he was a small boy. He turned, picked up the rifle that was by the door, cocked it, hung it over his shoulder, opened the door and stepped out, looking behind him as his family called out well wishes.

He was on his way. His only company was hibernating trees, blinding white snow and the whistling wind. The snow crackled under his feet with each step. In some places his foot would punch through the freezing layer of ice that lay on top of the snow, and he would sink almost knee-deep. This would be a long hard trip, but each step brought him closer to Nikolayevska. So on he went with the wind gusting into his eyes and drying them, causing him to blink. He tried not to dwell on the severe trip but on the reward of hearing his mother's and brothers' voices.

After a long tiring walk, his first dreaded night was almost upon him. "Oh, God, where am I going to sleep tonight and keep warm?" No sooner had the prayer left his lips when he spotted a pine tree with long low branches. "That will keep the wind off me," he said quietly and started toward it.

It was time to eat. He lit a fire and then gathered snow in the pot. As the water boiled, he sat and warmed himself by the fire. The jerky soup smelled so inviting, but he was nervous about letting it sit too long. It might invite the nasty wolves that he had been worrying about. Quickly he put on his right glove, picked up the pot, blew on its wonderful contents and took small sips. Delicious! The dried bread dipped into the honey was better still. When he finished he sat quietly by the fire, looked up at the stars and admired their beauty. He made up his mind to sit by the fire until it burned itself out. All was quiet. Even the wind ceased.

Suddenly a still small voice broke the silence. It was speaking into his heart. "Take cheer, my child, you are not abandoned or forsaken. I am with you now and always will be. Keep going. I will show you where to find shelter each night and keep you safe."

Alixey's eyes welled up. The God who created all the stars and everything around him was taking care of him. Who was this God? All his life he had had been told that God was fierce. He was not fierce at all. He seemed kind, gentle, loving and caring. His parents had taught him to observe the Law of Moses. Jesus died for the people of the Old Testament, but they had to observe the law to get into heaven. But if God were so fierce, why would He care so much about his safety and comfort? No one would believe that God spoke to him. He would keep it to himself lest they excommunicate him from the church.

Alixey was feeling the warmth from the fire. His eyelids started to feel heavy. He took the bearskin blanket from the pack and crawled underneath the pine tree, pulling his pack with him. He could feel the difference already; the pine needles were a barrier from the cold. He could hear the occasional gusts of wind, but they were not getting to him. While on his hands and knees, he stretched the blanket on the ground, sat down on it and pulled off his boots. It felt good to be able to wiggle his toes. He had to be good to his feet; they needed to take him through the mountains to the Altai valley. He lay down on one end of the blanket and, grasping the other side, rolled himself up in it. Still wearing his scarf and coat, feeling toasty warm, he was soon asleep.

A clump of snow fell crashing to the ground when a gust of wind blew against it. Alixey opened his eyes to see what had just happened. It was daylight. He didn't remember falling asleep, but it was time to get up, eat something and get going. He unrolled himself, sat up and pulled his cold boots on his warm feet. He got down on his hands and knees and crawled out from under the tree, bringing the blanket and pack along. After folding the blanket and stuffing it into the pack, he pulled some jerky out of his bag and slowly chewed it while taking time to wake up completely.

He had a lot more walking to do and was glad that so far there had been no sign of wolves, not even tracks. He checked his rifle to make sure it was ready to be fired if the need arose.

Picking up his pack and putting it on, then pulling the rifle strap over his left shoulder, he started off. He was missing his wife and daughters but glad that, God willing, he would be seeing his mother and brothers. Someday soon they would be reunited. The thought made the loneliness evaporate, and he started to walk faster.

Some nights he slept between rocks to keep the wind off. Other nights he found shallow caves. Each night there was a provision for him, and still there was no sign of wolves.

Alixey had been in Russia three days, each step bringing him closer to Nikolayevska. Tired of the crackling of the snow, his eyes strained from the bright reflection off it, he was ready for the walking to end. He wondered how the village had changed. He did not even want to see his old house lest he give in to the urge to burn it down. At last he found himself in the forest where he used to play as a young boy, almost to the frozen river, his family just on the other side. Tired and hungry—he had had to ration his food to be sure he didn't run out—he knew he would not need to spend another night in the woods and that usually no wolves came this close to civilization. He needed to hide his rifle and pack somewhere in case he was spotted. Remembering a hollow tree nearby, he headed toward it to stash his things.

There it was, just the same after all these years. He got down on his knees, pulled the bearskin out of his pack, rolled his rifle up in it and pushed it into the hollow of the tree along with his pack. He turned and headed toward his mother's converted chicken coop. He had to wait until dark before he could cross the road over the river into the village.

Seeing a pine tree that had branches hanging low from the weight of the snow, he decided to sit under it and to wait out the daylight.

Suddenly, out of nowhere a loud intimidating voice called out, "Halt! What are you doing here?"

Quickly spinning around, he saw two soldiers on their horses. They wore their army hats pulled low on their foreheads and long army coats with scarves wrapped around their necks and mouths. All he could see were cold black eyes.

Being quick-witted, he pointed to the air and answered, "My friends and I are trapping rabbits for their fur."

"What friends?" the soldier barked.

"This on my right is Anatoly and on my left is Misha," Alixey answered.

"And who are you?" the soldier asked.

"I am Petro, the son of Vasili."

The soldier laughed at him, looked over at his partner and pointed to his head and twirled his finger, a gesture used to describe someone who is mentally ill. "He is no threat. Let him go," he added.

The soldiers quickly rode back toward the village.

"This must be their patrol," Alixey said under his breath as he crawled under the pine tree. His body was tired; he was ready to eat a warm meal and sleep in a soft bed. The ground was cold and hard, and he shivered. The exposed part of his face was wind-burned and sore to the touch. His ordeal was almost over. Without even noticing, he dropped off to sleep.

A dog started barking, and Alixey was startled awake. He opened his eyes and stretched his legs, sore from all the walking. He climbed out from under the tree. It was very dark; the full moon had not yet risen. His mother and brothers now lived close to the soldiers' post; a dark night was a good thing.

He started for the river and carefully side-stepped down the steep bank. He slipped, landed on his left side, and slid down to the iced-over river. He rolled over on his back, lay there a while too exhausted and sore to move just yet and looked up at the stars.

Finally some of his strength returned. He gingerly got up and walked across the ice to the opposite bank. Careful not to slip again, he climbed the bank and was cheered—even though it was draped only with a shabby old tablecloth—to see light coming from the window of his family's little home.

The smell of chimney smoke hung in the air. That meant warmth and hot food. The frozen snow crackled as he started walking toward the house in which he grew up and from which his mother and brothers had been evicted. The large windows had no curtains; there was light in every room. He could see soldiers, singing loudly, sitting around a rectangular table with what looked like vodka bottles. He did not recognize the song.

Alixey would have loved to burn down the house. His father had built the house with sweat and blisters. Now these men were drinking, singing, and living in it while his mother and brothers lived in a chicken coop. Anger surged through him. He wanted so badly to go kick in the door and tell them off. But he would never actually do such a stupid thing; he would sneak in and back out with his family and nothing more.

Alixey crept up to his mother's door and gently knocked.

"Who is there?" Daved's voice called out.

"It's me, Alixey," he answered quietly.

He heard footsteps rapidly approaching. The door swung open. Daved stood at the door, his mama and Petro behind him. All three greeted him with tears of joy. Daved grabbed him and quickly pulled him into the house. His mother, crying out his name again and again, pushed both boys aside and fell into his arms. She asked him if this were real or a dream.

"Mama, it's me, Alixey. I'm tired, cold and hungry."

She stepped back, pulled a chair back from the table and told him to sit so she could serve him dinner.

Alixey pulled off his mittens, unraveled his scarf and took off his hat and coat. The warm air all around him felt wonderful. The smell of the stew his mother set before him was even better; so was the soft bread. "Oy, this is a feast for a czar!" Alixey said as he started eating.

"Eat, my son. Eat all you want. I have more," his mama told him in a soothing voice.

Alixey ate his fill and drank a tall cup of milk. Petro and Daved visited with him while he ate, and his mother fixed a bed for him on the bread oven. Constructed of bricks, it was six feet long, four feet wide and three feet high. It was nice and toasty warm and served for a bed for Petro. Alixey climbed up, pulled off his boots and lay down still wearing his sweater. He pulled the blanket up and was asleep as soon as his head hit the pillow.

6

Preparations

After the lights were out in the post next door, and all was quiet, Daved and Petro went to the barn to prepare the sleigh and horses and to gather all their warm blankets and bearskins for the long cold trip the next night or the night after.

Daved and Petro had something to tell Alixey regarding Anya's brother. They knew he would take Anya's family to China once he found out what had happened during his absence. So once their own sleigh and horses were ready, they went to do the same for Feodor and Fedosia, Anya's parents. Without waking them, the boys went straight to the barn and lit the lantern. Daved checked the horses. Well cared-for, these horses were fat and sleek, with smooth hooves and the shoes on just like they should be. The runners on the sleigh were a little rough. Around the village they would do fine, but they could split on a long trip. Petro started rummaging around the shelves looking for a file to smooth them.

Feodor and his wife were in bed sleeping when he heard noise coming from the direction of the barn. Getting out of bed, he hurried down the stairs to look out the kitchen window. He saw light coming from the barn. It couldn't be his son. Was he being robbed? What did they want? He pulled on his boots, put on his coat, hat and scarf, then picked up his rifle and made sure it was loaded and ready. He opened the door, stepped outside and slammed the door shut so that whoever was in the barn would know they were in trouble. Perhaps it was one of the gang members that had shot his son. What did they want, his horses? Well, they would not get them. The soldiers had taken his stronger horses. These two were all he had left, and he was keeping them. He rushed into the barn with his rifle ready to aim and shoot. His jaw was clenched, his teeth locked and grinding.

Daved and Petro were startled at his appearance.

"What are you doing here?" he asked, relieved to find friends and not foes, and lowered his rifle.

"Petro, why is my sleigh upside down and why are you fixing the runners?"

Petro was going to reply, but Daved beat him to it. "Alixey is back. He is here to take us back to China with him. When he finds out what happened to Simon, he will not let you stay here. So we are here to make sure your sleigh and horses are ready for travel. The runners are a little rough so we are smoothing them."

Feodor set his rifle in a corner and sat on a wooden box by the wall. "How are they doing there?" he asked them.

"Well," answered Petro, "when Alixey arrived he was very tired and hungry. Mama fed him and now he is asleep. But when he wakes in the morning, we will find out. He walked all the way here."

"Oy, he walked—all the way? Yes, that explains why he's tired and hungry. I know my Anya will be worried sick about him." Then with a distant stare and a half smile he continued, "This does not feel like home anymore. This village is more like a prison. More like a death trap." He looked back at Daved and Petro and quietly said, "China. Good, I will talk to my wife in the morning. I know she is not happy here either. But what about Simon? He is too weak to make such a journey sitting up."

Daved spoke up. "Oh, that won't be a problem. We'll make it just as comfortable as if he was home in bed. We'll make a soft warm bed for him in the back of the sleigh. He will be able to sit up or lie down."

Feodor was deeply touched by the love and caring of these people, who would go out of their way to do all this for him and his family.

"Feodor, go back in the house and get some sleep. We will complete what we have started and go home ourselves. We'll tell our brother we have talked, and I know he will be coming to see you."

Feodor turned, pushed open the barn door and stepped out, shutting it behind him. The snow crackled beneath his boots as he approached the house. He slowly opened the door to keep it from creaking, stepped in and gently closed it behind him. He wasn't expecting to see his wife by the kitchen window. "Why are you up?" he asked.

"I heard the front door slam and came down to see what's going on. Why is there a light in the barn?"

Feodor hesitated by the door, and then asked her to have a seat at the table. "Daved and Petro are preparing our sleigh," he told her as he started toward the table himself.

"Why are they doing that?"

"Alixey is back from China. He is here to take the boys and their mother there. He doesn't know about Simon yet." He pulled a chair out from the table and sat down beside his wife. "We need to talk," he continued. "The boys seem to think that Alixey will not leave without us."

"Oh, so that is why the sleigh is being prepared," Fedosia said, and she slowly nodded her head. She stood up, walked over

41

to the stove, picked up a box of matches and lit the candle in the center of the table. The full moon gave some light through the window. But they had serious talking to do. She needed the light.

The candlelight showed the pain in her eyes. First her son was shot by a murderous gang, then while barely hanging on to life, his wife left him. He was so brokenhearted that he almost gave up the fight but since then had recovered enough to know that with time he would be fine.

Feodor knew this trip would be hard on Fedosia. First the bitter cold and the fear of wolves attacking. Or, what if something happened to the horses? And many other what-ifs. But it was time to do something. This village was no longer a safe haven for them. They had the soldiers to contend with, and the murderous gangs that ran from village to village. Even the soldiers feared the gangs; they did not have enough manpower to tangle with them, so they pretended there was no problem. Feodor loved this ebony-eyed woman. Her eyes, always so welcoming. When she looked at someone, it was as if he or she were the only person in the world. The way her jet black hair framed her face. She was so beautiful and amazing. Always working beside him without complaint, happy and having time for anyone who needed help. But of late she was like a wilting flower, and now this trip.

Finally she spoke up. "So, when do we leave? And what about Oseph and Zenya? I know the girls are in other villages and it would take too much to contact them. We can just write each of them a letter and send it with the mail carrier. He can take it to them in the spring. Should we wake Oseph and Zenya now?" she asked.

"No need." They heard Oseph's voice from around the corner. "We have been listening to your conversation. We heard the door slam, then someone walk down the creaky stair, so we came down to see what was going on."

"Well, then, come in here and sit with us," Feodor requested. "Now that you've heard, what do you think?"

Oseph and Zenya walked in and sat like Feodor wanted. Oseph looked over at his wife and answered, "I don't know. I defer to my wife. I don't know if she would be willing to leave her parents behind." He loved his Zenya; she meant the world to him. If she preferred to stay, then that is what he was prepared to do.

"Well, Zenya," her mother-in-law asked. "What is your thought in this whole matter?"

"I would miss my parents very much, but I do not want to have my children and raise them in this cage. I prefer freedom. I want to go with my husband to China."

"Very well," rang out Feodor's voice. His hand almost slapped the table. He stopped himself. It would have been a sign of disrespect. This was where they ate their God-given meals. "All right, we leave with Alixey." He stood up and went to the window; the light was still on in the barn. "Petro and Daved are still in the barn." He fell silent as if trying to think of something else to say.

"What is it, Papa?" Oseph asked. "We have only one sleigh and two horses. How will we all fit and bring what is needed?" Oseph was looking down at the table when a smile flashed across his face. "I know! We can use the reindeer, Bobka and Domka, to pull the sleigh."

"The reindeer?" Feodor asked in a squeaky voice.

"Yes, Papa, why not? They are hand-raised, and they pull the sleigh on our hunting trips. They can pull heavy loads. Daved and Petro used them last winter to haul wood. I know they can do it."

"All right, but what will they pull?"

43

Suddenly Daved's voice came from the other side of the window. "What about Vasili? He had a nice sleigh in the barn under all the hay."

Feodor walked over to the door, opened it, and invited Daved and Petro in.

"We saw the light coming from the window and decided to let you know the sleigh is ready," Daved informed them. He and Petro were bundled up; all that could be seen was their eyes.

"What did you say about Vasili's sleigh?" Feodor asked.

"I know there is a sleigh in Vasili's barn, buried under some hay. Petro and I helped him bring in his hay last summer shortly before he left. He had so much he ran out of room, and we piled the extra over the sleigh. I'm sure he won't mind if we borrow it. He may even see you riding around in it somewhere in China," Daved chuckled.

"Well, if you are sure it is still there, go get it while we still have the cloak of night," replied Feodor.

Oseph ran up the stairs, dressed and came down again bundled up for the freezing cold, and the three of them stepped out and disappeared in the dark.

Feodor closed the door behind them. He pulled on his hat, wrapped his scarf around his neck, mouth and nose, picked up his mittens and left to go get firewood. His wife would need the bread oven and the wood stove to prepare enough food for the journey.

Fedosia and Zenya went upstairs and dressed. There was a lot of work to be done. When they returned, Feodor was on his knees in front of the stove starting a fire.

While he went out to get more wood for the brick oven, Zenya went to the root cellar for a jar of honey and came up just as her father-in-law returned with the wood. She gave the honey to Fedosia and went back for more. Little by little she packed it all out of the cellar. Honey was money; you could buy all sorts of goods for honey, even livestock. Feodor and Fedosia loved that girl; she was level-headed and loved their son.

Fedosia made large batches of bread dough in two mixing tubs and pastry dough in a third.

Feodor went out again. This time he brought in two large buckets of venison jerky from the smoke house. Before long he heard voices in the barnyard. He was sure the boys did not find the sleigh. They were back too soon. If they were pulling and pushing it, they would have been gone longer. Disappointed, he stepped out to console the three guys. His eyes caught a glimpse of the sleigh and his disappointment vanished. "How did you get it here so fast?"

"It practically pulled itself, Papa," Oseph answered.

The three stood there covered with bits of hay, trying to brush it off with their mittens.

"The sleigh is so well balanced, it doesn't pull to the right or left, it just goes in the direction it's being pulled. Bobka and Domka will have no trouble pulling it," added Daved.

"Very good," snickered Petro, "Four Altai horses and two reindeer are going to take all of us to China. Someday I will be able to tell the story to my children."

They did not know at that moment that it was God's plan to get them out of that valley. Something was going on deep in the ground, of which they were unaware. They had been praying and asking to be freed from their oppressors, and God had made a way where there seemed to be no way. They knew of God but knew nothing of His heart or of how much He loved them; they did not know that He was with them right where they were and would always be there for them. There was not a single Bible in the village. But they knew He was their helper. He was all they had. This gave them courage and strength.

45

Axiniya, Alixey's mother, was starting to worry about her boys. They had been gone a while. Were they all right? Suddenly she heard them kicking the door jamb to knock the snow off their boots.

The noise woke Alixey, but he did not mind. It was good to hear the sound. They were his family. He just lay there and listened to the sounds and smelled the familiar smells.

The first question their mother asked them was, "Why were you gone so long?"

"We did some work on Feodor's sleigh, then went to get Vasili's sleigh for the trip."

Alixey heard all that was said and sat up.

"Did we wake you?" his mother asked.

"It's all right, Mama," he answered, giving her a very endearing look.

"Now what did you say about Feodor's sleigh? And I also heard something about Vasili's sleigh," he added, directing this at Daved.

His mother interrupted before Daved could reply. "There is something we need to tell you." She hesitated for a moment, then continued, "Simon was hunting up north of here. He shot a deer and had just loaded it up onto the horse in front of him when a bullet ripped through his upper left arm. He looked back and saw who shot him. Thuggees—they prided themselves on their kills. Well, Simon was only wounded, and he knew they would pursue him until they succeeded. Holding onto the deer, he rode like the wind. He lost a lot of blood. His coat sleeve caught the blood, or else the thugs could have followed him up to the house. When he rode up, Feodor was coming out of the barn. Simon fell off his horse. Over and over he kept saying, 'Hide me!' Well, they knew it must have been the thuggees and that they'd be looking for him. They couldn't hide him in the house or barn; he would be found, so they pulled the horse trough aside, quick-like, and dug a long trench with picks and shovels. The women shoveled the dirt into buckets, carried it to the river and threw it in the water. They wrapped him in a blanket and laid him in the trench. They put boards across it and pulled the trough back over it and overfilled it with hay. They laid the deer in among the reindeer. The thugs searched the whole village, but even when they came to Feodor's house they did not find him or the deer. In the meantime he lost a lot of blood."

"Where were the soldiers this whole time?" Alixey asked.

"The soldiers." His mama raised her voice and pointed in that direction. "The soldiers will not tangle with them. The only thing they're good for is throwing people out of their homes."

"But wait, here's the sad part. His wife left him. Said it was too much for her to handle. Feodor loaded her in his sleigh under great protest and took her to her parents'. Those murderers're still out there somewhere."

"Did the bullet pass through or did it have to be taken out?" Alixey asked.

"It went through but left a large hole. He lost a lot of blood and a few days later a fever set in. He developed an infection. Svetlana brought him herbs. Some she made into tea; others were applied to the wound."

Alixey loved Anya's family. He had been concerned about his friend Simon. They had bonded after he married Anya. He could not leave them; he had to take them also.

"How is he doing now?" Alixey asked.

"Weak," answered his mother. "The loss of blood and the fever took it out of him."

"Well, then, we won't leave without Simon and his family."

"Good," Petro blurted out, slapping his thigh. That was his gesture of excitement. "Oseph and Zenya are going also, and Bobka and Domka are pulling the sleigh."

"Bobka and Domka?" Both Alixey and his mother spoke at the same time.

"Yeah," Petro answered in a chuckle. "Bobka and Domka. They're pets, and we don't want to leave them behind."

"Think those animals can pull a sleigh?" asked their mother.

"I know they can," answered Petro. "They pulled a sleigh full of firewood not very long ago, Mama."

Alixey climbed down from his warm bed, stretched and yawned. He looked around at their very cramped little home. They had cleaned it, built the brick oven and put in a cook stove. The small bed at the opposite end must be where Mama slept. There was rolled up bedding under the table. "So who sleeps under the table?" he asked.

"That's my bedroom, dear brother," answered Daved.

"Well, don't get used to it. Tomorrow we might leave," replied Alixey with a smile. He picked up his boots, went to a chair, sat down and pulled them on.

"Where are you going?" his mama asked.

"Not far, just to the outhouse," he answered. Pulling on his hat and putting on his coat, he wrapped the scarf around his nose and mouth and stepped out into the cold.

7

Earthquake

Walking through the barnyard, Alixey suddenly felt the earth move ever so slightly under his feet. *I must be really tired*, he thought. On his way back to the house the earth really started to move. *Earthquake!* he thought. Another strong jolt immediately came after the first one and knocked him off his feet. He tried to get up but the jolts continued. There he was, helpless, now on his hands and knees. He wasn't wearing his gloves. The jolting caused him to slide from side to side, and he could feel the sharp edges of the ice scraping his hands. His knees seemed to be protected by his long coat.

"Mama, Petro, Daved," he heard himself say just above a whisper. "Are they all right?"

The jolting continued. Still on his hands and knees, he started to crawl. His hands were numbed by the ice. Suddenly everything became still. He slowly got to his feet and walked over to the door. His mother and brothers were in the doorway. All three were shaken up but okay. Alixey was grateful for that. He reached out and hugged all three of them.

His mother tried to appear brave, but her rapid breathing gave her away. "It's okay, Mama. I was frightened also."

Suddenly they heard voices coming from the post behind them. He gently pushed everyone inside and pushed the door shut. He did not want to be discovered.

Mama's pots and pans and some of the metal plates were on the floor. He needed to wash his hands before he could help her pick them up. He took off his hat, scarf, and coat and hung them on the coat rack next to the door. He walked over to the hand-washing bucket, which was on its side, its contents spilled on the floor. He set it upright. The water pot was between the stove and the wall. Much of the water had splashed out, but enough remained to wash his hands. Alixey picked up the bar of soap off the floor and asked Petro to pour water over his hands. He rubbed the soap between his hands and worked up a lather, then set the soap on the shelf above the water bucket. He rubbed his hands together to get them clean. His hands burned from all the scratches. Petro poured more water until the soapy feeling was gone. He then wiped his hands on the towel hanging on a nail above the bucket.

Daved had picked up the pots, pans, and plate. His mother wiped up the water on the floor.

"Wow, that did not take long," remarked Alixey.

"When you don't have much, it doesn't take long to pick it up," Mama replied.

The large pan of bread had danced across the table but not over the edge.

Alixey checked the stove pipe. It was completely intact. The bread oven had no cracks in it. They could proceed as planned. That was one headache they did not need.

Suddenly there was a knock at the door. Alixey dove under the table, and his mother pulled the tablecloth down low to conceal him. "Who's there?" she called out.

"It's Samsun," the voice called back. He was a neighbor and friend. Alixey wasn't sure if he could still be trusted. There probably was a bounty on his head, and would his old friend be greedy enough to collect it?

Mama opened the door halfway.

"Are you all right? We are going door to door checking on everyone. That was a strong earthquake; the ground opened up a little over by the big house. I would have fallen into it, but I saw it just in time by the moonlight. I am going out to Feodor and Fedosia's next."

"Daved and Petro are getting ready to go there right now. So you don't have to." She did not want anyone to see the sleigh and get suspicious.

"We are leaving in a few minutes," called Daved.

"Well, good night, then," Samsun told them quietly. He stepped back, turned and left.

His mother closed the door as Alixey climbed out from under the table and headed toward the coat rack. She knew where he was going. "Be careful, son," she pleaded.

Alixey put on his warm coat, hat and scarf. He turned to his mama and kissed her cheek. His brothers were heading toward the coat rack as well.

"I'm going alone. You stay here with Mama. I will be back before dawn. Get some rest. We will start getting ready when I return."

He cracked the door open and peered out, then stepped out and closed it behind him. Looking around to see if anyone was watching, he quickly set off. His legs were still sore from his long walk, but the more he walked the better they felt. The wind was brutal; it whistled continually. Some nights were worse than others; this was one of them. He had to bow his head to keep it out of his eyes. The snow crackled on the walk. He would never forget that sound.

Finally he could see light in Feodor and Fedosia's house. It would be warm there. The house was smaller than his and Anya's. He had built his own house big, planning to have a large family. Now it wasn't his anymore...but he was done being upset; he was letting it go. His father and mother also had built a big house in the hope of having lots of children, but his father died before his dream was realized. The size of his father's house interested Stalin; it was large enough to use as a military station. And his house would be a school.

Alixey realized how tightly his teeth were clenched.

Deliberately he made himself relax. He would have been happy if that house had collapsed during the earthquake. All of his and his father's hard work was taken from them. A gust of wind hit him in the eyes as if to remind him of what was going on right now.

At last he was on the doorstep. He gently knocked and right away he heard voices. Feodor's voice asked, "Who's there?"

"It's Alixey," he answered. The door flew open. Both of Anya's parents were at the door. They greeted him with great joy laced with sadness. Feodor gestured to him to come inside. As he came into the house, Fedosia grabbed him and hugged him tightly. When she was finished, his father-in-law did the same.

It was tradition to call your spouse's parents Mama and Papa, never by their first names. "Mama, Papa, how are you and how is Simon?" he asked. "I heard Oseph and Zenya are also coming," he continued.

"We are all right. Simon is still a little weak but is finally able to get up and down the stairs," answered Fedosia.

Alixey took off his hat and scarf. They motioned him into the dining room to sit at the table. Fedosia had made a big pot of herb tea. She poured him a cup, set a jar of honey on the table to sweeten it, then quickly sliced some bread to dip into the honey.

Alixey looked around to assess what sort of damage had been done by the earthquake. Judging by the soot all over the wall behind it, the stovepipe seemed to have fallen but had been put back. The oven showed no cracks and by the look of things everything had been picked up. He reached for his herb tea and saw the venison jerky on a plate in front of him. He had been living on jerky for days and would be eating more on their way back to China, but being polite, he took a piece and took a small bite off the edge.

"I'm sorry, but this is all I have to offer right now. Everything ended up on the floor, even the bread and pastry dough," Fedosia told him.

"Alixey, is that you?" Simon called out from the family room.

Alixey jumped up and ran to him. "Simon, my dear friend and brother-in-law," he said as he entered the room where Simon was sitting. He saw a frail, thin, pale man trying hard to control his emotions.

Simon stood up and Alixey gently hugged him, being very careful of his left arm, which was in a sling.

Alixey stepped back to take a look at the arm. "Are you able to move it?" he asked.

"Yes, but right now I would rather not. It is still very sore."

"Then you rest it, my dear friend. Have your family told you we are all leaving?"

"Yes, they have," answered Simon as a shadow of sadness covered his face, and he blinked back tears.

"You heard that Nadiya left me?" Simon was fighting back tears.

"Yes, I have," answered Alixey. "I know you love her very much, and I don't know how to comfort you."

"She wasn't happy here, and she was embarrassed that we have no children. She was just waiting for the right opportunity to leave. And this was the one."

"Somehow, with the help of God and friends, someday I will be happy again." Fatigued, he sat down on a bench that was along the wall. He hung his head and started to weep.

Alixey sat silently next to him. No words could ease Simon's pain.

Then Simon spoke up again. "I used to be strong and vigorous, the first one out the door to go and do the work that needed to be done. Now I have been reduced to this. I could not even hang on to my wife. Am I so repulsive?"

Alixey knew his friend was in deep emotional pain. All he could do was let him vent. He just sat in silence wishing for healing words, but there were none. He had felt this pain when his own father died and he was left with all the responsibilities. His mother and two brothers became dependent on him. He had had to grow up very fast.

As Simon and Alixey sat in the family room, an aftershock rocked the house, but it did not last long. Fedosia let out a scream. They jumped up and hurried into the kitchen, where Fedosia was hanging on to the table.

Simon walked up to her and put his right arm around her as she shook. "Mama, it is only an aftershock. We will have a few more before everything settles down. They taught us this in school, Mama. It means the earth underneath is settling."

She turned and looked at Simon. "As long as we are together I will be fine. I am just hoping we can leave here tonight without getting caught."

"We will. God is watching over us. We will get out without being caught," Alixey assured her.

Pulled from the Ashes: Earthquake

Suddenly Feodor came in through the door, all bundled up; he had been in the barn milking the cow. He set the bucket on the floor in case of another aftershock. "Alixey, I heard loud voices and screaming coming from the village. You had better go and see what is going on."

Alixey grabbed his hat and scarf and headed for the door.

"May God be with you, Alixey," Simon called out after him.

"May God be with you too, my friend," Alixey called back.

He stepped out to see the dawn just starting to light up the eastern hills. He quickly put on his hat and wrapped his scarf around his neck, mouth, and nose. He reached into his pockets, pulled out his mittens and put them on. He could hear what Feodor had been talking about. He went from a quick step to a run. He had to be careful; the frozen snow was a little slippery, and if he fell, it would not be as forgiving as the ground.

Finally he reached the outskirts of the village. He could not see the house his father built. He felt as if he had been struck by lightning. Where was it? His arms and feet felt heavy. He stopped and stared. Were his eyes deceiving him? Why could he not seethe house? Again he started to run. As he drew closer, he saw people in their heavy coats, scarves, and hats, milling around where the house had been. The window in his family's cabin was broken and some of the roof had slid off. "Mama, Petro, Daved," he heard himself call out, his voice cracking. As he drew nearer, not caring if anyone saw him, he discovered that the big house had sunk out of sight into the ground and collapsed. He ran into the cabin. Empty! Frantically he started calling for his family.

"We're here," Daved called back. "In the barn."

Turning quickly, he ran in their direction. All three were standing just inside the barn.

"What happened?" he panted.

"Well," Daved answered, "the earth began to shake when suddenly there was a loud crack coming from behind our cabin. Then the window blew out. We grabbed our coats and ran outside. Before we knew it, the roof started to slide off, so we came out here to the barn. After the shaking stopped, we went to check on the cabin and noticed the big house had sunk into the ground and collapsed. We don't know how the soldiers are doing. That's a lot of lumber to be falling down."

"Why did the house sink down, I wonder?" asked Alixey.

"Wow, you should see the big hole," spoke up Petro. "The ground underneath opened, and the house just fell in."

Samsun, a neighbor, said something about the ground opening up by the house.

"The aftershock must have caused it to open all the way," continued Petro. Daved just stood there nodding his head.

Alixey took a deep breath, let it out and said, "If you had been living in it, that could have been you." He looked up at the ceiling of the barn. He thanked God for His mysterious ways while his family agreed with him.

"Well, we'd better go see if we can help in any way," Alixey continued.

"But what if you are recognized?" asked his mother.

"That's not important. Those men have families too. We need to help if we can," answered Alixey. Daved and Alixey started toward the rubble.

His mother reached out and took hold of Petro's arm. "Stay here, my son. There are already a lot of people coming and going. We will stay right here and watch."

Daved and Alixey walked over to the opening, where two men were calling to the soldiers. They waited in case someone responded so they could be on hand to help with the rescue.

"Hello!" called out one of the men crawling around on the rubble. "Can anyone hear me? Please respond and we will help."

There was only silence.

"Alixey, is that you?" a woman called excitedly.

He quickly turned toward the voice. It was Domna, Samsun's wife and long-time friend of Anya's. "I would recognize those blue eyes anywhere! We thought you and your family had been arrested and taken away. That is what the soldiers told us."

Alixey and Daved both stood silently searching for the right response.

Then Alixey went over to her and hugged her. Domna responded in kind. He thought she wasn't going to let go of him. Finally she loosened her grip and let go. Alixey took a step back and slowly shook his head.

"No, Domna. Anya, the girls and I have fled to China. Vasili and Masha are there also. We haven't seen them yet but I'm sure they are not too far from us. There is a lot of land along the Chubaroy River. Enough land and timber for a whole village. The grass is tall and green, and the people there are friendly and welcoming. Anya and I bought a large piece of land. We are starting over. The best part of all, Stalin has no power there. It's called freedom and no fear of losing it."

"Why have you come back here, Alixey?" Domna asked. "What if you are arrested? What about Anya and the girls?"

"I'm here to take my family and Anya's family out of this place to China, where we can all be together. But before we continue this conversation I need to tell Petro and Mama something."

He turned and walked over to them. "Petro, go hitch the horse to the sleigh, please. And Mama, my darling, go and gather everything for our trip. Petro will bring the sleigh to the cabin, and I will be there shortly to help load."

He turned to ask Daved to help and could not find him. "Daved!" he called out.

"Down here," Daved replied. His voice sounded muffled.

Alixey realized his brother had climbed down to the wreckage. "Come on up and help Mama," Alixey called to him.

"I'm coming!" he heard Daved reply.

The two men who were down below also climbed out. One of them called out to the people who were now gathered around the barn by Alixey.

"We don't think anyone survived. It makes no sense to continue."

Sadness fell on the people. Even though they were their oppressors, they were still human beings with souls that had to face eternity.

Alixey could see the excitement in the gathered crowd, but they remained quiet while he continued to give directions to his family.

Yakov was one of the men who had been down in the rubble. He walked up to Alixey, not saying a word. All that could be seen was his eyes. Alixey could tell he was grinning. He suddenly grabbed Alixey around his waist and gave him a bear hug. Not his usual hugging ritual to his fishing buddy, this time he hugged him so hard he lifted him off the ground and slightly shook him from side to side. Finally he let out a loud "Yahoo! My Alixey, you are back—you are back!" His voice was full of excitement. He set him down, but his grin remained.

"We were told you were in prison," he blurted out.

"No, my friend, my three girls and I now live in China along the Chubaroy River."

Daved was standing silently at Alixey's side. "What do you want me to do?" he asked.

"We need to hitch the horses to the sleigh and have it pulled to the front of the cabin."

"Mama's in there packing. We need to go and stay with Feodor and Fedosia. I will be there in a few minutes to help."

Daved walked to the barn to see if Petro needed help.

Alixey turned back to Yakov and the crowd, and said, "We escaped during the night. We crossed the river by the ford and traveled south. It took many days. It was during the summer and was much easier. We bought property—lots of it. It was not expensive," he continued. "There is much more land, enough for a large village. I settled my family into a dugout, a house that is underground. It suits our family. There is a lot of timber and plenty of fish in the river. In the spring I am going to start building a house, and Anya and I will live out our dream again. We will have our big family and raise them in freedom."

"How did you get back here?" asked Domna.

"I walked. I slept under low evergreen branches or in caves between rocks. I ate bread cubes and drank jerky soup. The trip was very difficult but to have my family all together, I would do it many times over," explained Alixey.

"When are you leaving here?" asked Yakov.

"Today, as soon as everyone is ready. I am taking my in-laws also. We are taking three sleighs. I was going to wait until tonight but am feeling an urgency. It feels as if tonight will be too late."

"If we give you gold, will you buy us property?" piped up Samsun. "I think it won't be too long before we are searched, and have it taken from us anyway. We may as well buy land in China with it."

Resounding agreement came from the crowd.

"So, anyone who wants to send gold for land in China give it to Alixey. We will have him buy up all the land available along the river. We will write down who gave how much and then divide the land when we all get there," continued Samsun.

Alixey was filled with joy. He could not wait to bring this news to his wife. "When will you be coming?" he asked.

"In the spring, as soon as the snow thaws. Some of us have little children. We cannot put them through the hardship of traveling in this cold. Shelter is also another factor. We can pitch tents in the spring." Nikolai, who was speaking, was the pastor of their church and mayor of the village. "Now, my friends, let's help these people leave here as soon as possible. They will need food for themselves and grain for their animals. And, of course, your gold." He said it with a chuckle. "I will write down the amount given by each family."

Everyone headed for their homes, and Alixey saw the sleigh sitting in front of the cabin. As he walked toward it, another sleigh came up the road at high speed. He had to take a second look. Domka and Bobka were pulling it.

"Whoa! Whoa!" called out Oseph, and the reindeer came to a stop.

"Well, what do you think, Alixey?" Oseph called out.

Seeing everything come together, Alixey chuckled with delight.

"Daved, Petro, Mama!" he called. "Come out here!"

They filed out the door and he waved them over. When they got to him, he pointed to the road. They saw Oseph sitting proudly in the sleigh.

"How do you like my ride?" he asked.

Mama didn't say a word. She just turned and went back into the cabin. Petro and Daved walked over to pet the reindeer.

Alixey called out to Oseph, "Notify your parents that we are leaving as soon as possible."

Oseph was so excited about the sleigh ride that he had not noticed the demolished house. Now he jumped down from the sleigh, handed the reins to Daved and ambled over a few steps to look at the rubble.

Alixey motioned for Oseph to come back and pointed out the roof of the cabin to him. "We are getting cold and will be over soon. Go tell your parents."

Oseph's eyes widened. He looked at the roof, then at his brother-in-law. "Wow!" finally came out of his mouth. "Is everyone all right?"

"Yes," nodded Alixey.

"How about the people that were in the house?" he said, pointing to the rubble.

"No one responded," Alixey replied. "It's a lot of weight to fall on someone."

"I will go home right away. By the way, aren't you worried that someone will see you?"

"Oh, I have been seen by the whole village, my dear brother-in-law. We need to get out of here. I'm sure there will be another patrol coming soon. They will be busy all night pulling that rubble out. We need to be gone before then. So do not unhitch the animals. In fact, hitch the horses to the other sleigh."

8

Back to China

Oseph wasted no time; he sprinted back to the sleigh and
thanked Daved for holding the reins. Climbing up, he turned the
reindeer around and raced back home.

Alixey watched him disappear from sight, turned and went
over to the cabin. About to start loading their belongings, he
heard women's voices outside. He stepped out to see several
ladies carrying armloads of food-filled baskets and clay jars. Not
far behind them were their husbands.

"We brought food for your trip," called out one of the
women. "We have bread, of course. Jelly-filled pastries, bagels,
jam for your bread, venison jerky, roasted chickens and ducks,
pickled cucumbers and tomatoes."

Alixey called his mother over. He thanked each one of them,
his mama now at his side. Seeing what was happening, she broke
into tears, as she and her son took the food from these generous
women and placed it into their family-sized sleigh. She hugged
and thanked each one in turn.

Then the men stepped up; each pulled out a leather pouch
from his pocket to inform Alixey that this was the gold from all
the villagers for land in their new country. Alixey took it from

them, shook their hands, and gave each one a quick hug. Excusing himself, he headed back into the cabin and started carrying out their belongings.

Finally everything was loaded and tied on. They were ready to go. The neighbors had left. Alixey and his family took one last look around. Once a paradise, now this was Stalin's hellhole.

They had a difficult trip ahead of them. Perhaps they would have to fight wolves. The more noise they made, the more attention they would attract.

Daved and Petro took the small woodpile apart and pulled out their blanket-wrapped rifle and ammunition from the hole underneath. After some checking, the boys were satisfied it was ready to fire.

Mama and Petro climbed in the back seat and covered themselves with blankets. Alixey and Daved climbed up on a seat. After covering themselves up, Mama led them in a prayer. "Most merciful God, full of grace and long-suffering, we need courage and safety to make this trip. We need your protection from the wolves and anything that would want to harm us. Help us to stay warm and grant us unity in Jesus' name, amen."

Alixey took the reins, got a strong grip, and snapped them. The horses gave a slight jerk and the sleigh began to move. The runners made a hollow sound as they slid over the frozen snow. They were finally on their way.

"Goodbye, Papa," Petro whispered, and he pulled his blanket up under his chin.

"Yes, goodbye," Alixey and Daved spoke up, their voices shrouded in sadness.

"You were a very good man, a great husband and father," their mother added through her own sadness as she wept quietly.

Alixey did not offer any words of comfort. He knew she needed to do this. He felt the same way. He looked over at Daved, who was morose and not saying a word to anyone.

Alixey quietly directed the horses toward his in-laws' home, while praying all of them would be gone before the patrol showed up. As he came around the bend, he could see the sleigh in the yard. They were still packing. Alixey brought his sleigh to a stop beside theirs and climbed down. Petro and Daved jumped down and went inside to offer to help. Feodor asked the boys to help Simon up into the sleigh. The back seat had been removed, and several blankets had been laid out and pillows piled up.

Simon walked down the front steps on his own but lacked the strength to climb onto the sleigh. Daved ran up to help. Petro also hurried out the door with a step stool and set it beside the sleigh. Simon stepped up onto the stool as Daved, who had climbed onto the sleigh, took hold of his hand and of his right arm above the elbow. With Daved pulling and Petro pushing from behind, Simon managed to get on the sleigh. He lay down on the waiting blankets and pillows as Daved jumped back down on the opposite side.

Simon was already bundled up in his long coat, scarf, and hat. Daved and Petro covered him up by rolling the ends of the blanket up over him. They made sure that he was comfortable before going back into the house for more supplies.

Finally all was in order. Feodor had his ammunition ready; he just needed his rifle. Looking around the barn, he remembered sadly when it had been filled with cows and horses but comforted himself with the thought that the next barn would be bigger. He picked up the rifle from the corner and thought back to the night before when Daved and Petro were preparing his horses and sleigh. He turned and left without a word; he wasn't going to shed any tears or say any goodbyes. These past few months had been terrible and he was ready to leave all that behind. Yes, he would miss his daughters. He had written a letter to each of them telling them of his destination and welcoming them to follow. Nikolai, his pastor, had instructions to send the letters when the mail carrier was active again.

Oseph and Zenya were covered in blankets, the reindeer and sleigh already pointed in the right direction. Feodor walked up to Alixey, already seated, to say that he thought that since Oseph and Zenya did not have a rifle, they should travel between them.

"I have a rifle hidden in the woods," Alixey informed him. "We will stop and pick it up along with my supplies. Oseph can use it. I will lead, you follow."

"Very good," Feodor agreed. He went over to his own sleigh, climbed up, covered himself with a blanket, and they were on their way. They went through the village toward the bridge, where several of their friends were gathered. As they started across, their friends called out goodbyes.

9

Winter

This had been the hardest winter that Anya had ever experienced. Her husband had left for Russia on foot, and she constantly asked herself, *Is he all right, and will we see him again?* The girls had been transplanted to this new country, and they missed their father, uncles, and grandparents. They did not yet know anyone here. They did not even have a church or school to attend. Anya was teaching Anuta at home, and Tanya was still too young. Constantly they asked, "When will Papa be home?"

Before long Anya had two unwanted companions: fear and depression. One told her that her husband had frozen to death. The other told her he had been captured and was now in prison. Sometimes they would tell her he had fallen victim to wolves. Either way, she was on her own with two helpless little girls. She could busy herself during the day and sometimes even be able to block out the voices. She had a cow to milk, two horses and several chickens to feed. But the nights were very long and difficult. The voices snapped at her like hungry wolves. Sleepless nights had become the norm. She could hide her tears during the day, but at night she would quietly sob until she fell asleep from exhaustion. There was no way of contacting Alixey, so she just endured.

Anuta could see how her mama had become withdrawn and how sometimes she would just stare off into space for long periods of time.

"Mama, please don't abandon us," Anuta pleaded with her. "Papa will be home soon. I had a dream that Papa and all my uncles and grandparents were riding on three sleighs. They are on their way home to us. So please hang on, dearest Mama, please hang on."

Anya felt words of hope coming from the mouth of a babe. Ashamed for falling so deeply into this melancholy, in that instant she made up her mind that she would expect him home. She would no longer be in agreement with the hopelessness that had stolen all the anticipation of the future about which she and her husband had talked. After all, that was why they had made this trip, and why he was gone at that very moment. "We are going to have a new life, so, fear and depression, you are not going to harass me any longer!" Anya exclaimed. When they tried, she would dwell on what their new house, barn and chicken coop would look like. She would focus on her beautiful daughters, and how happy they made her. Little by little, joy became her new friend and family member. Anya, for the first time since her husband left, finally had a great night of sleep. Her mind was clear and rested.

It was time to milk the cow. She hoped the chickens had left them a few eggs. As she opened the door to the barn and stepped in, the horses made a fuss as usual. She was in her long fur coat, a thick wool scarf around her head, nose and mouth. The horses had a natural instinct of fearing things they did not recognize. Alixey had always taken care of them. They were still getting used to the appearance of her long coat. "Settle down," she commanded, and recognizing her voice, they did. She went to the bags where the grain had been stored, saw holes in the lower sections of the bags, and knew right away that they had a problem with rats. If enough of them got together, they could eat all the grain.

She searched along the woodwork of the barn to find where the rats were gaining entrance. Finally, she found that they had chewed through a seam in the wood of the wall. Anya went out to the woodpile, picked out several pieces that would fit snugly over the hole and piled them against it. Now she was sure they could not enter there. She knew rats. Now that they knew about the grain, they would start trying to make new entrances. She had to keep an eye on the grain. "I guess snow and freezing wind is not enough; now I have to battle rats, too," she said to herself. Upon closer inspection of the grain, she found that the rats had eaten quite a bit. The cows had enough hay, but she was unsure that the grain remaining would feed the chickens and horses all winter. Trying to be level-headed and not emotional, she sat down on a toolbox, found her voice and started praying. "Merciful God, the rats have eaten the grain and they will be back. I don't have any means of trapping them. Please give me wisdom on what to do." She waited a while but decided He wasn't going to answer.

After a short silence she got up and opened the door to the stall to let the cow and horses go to the river for a drink. She picked up the ax, went to the barn door and opened it. The horses and cow knew that it was time to go and followed her to the river for a drink. She walked ahead of them on the cleared trail. The water hole had frozen over as usual. Anya swung the ax and hit the ice. The ice shattered and the pieces fell into the water and were washed away while the animals took turns drinking. When they were done, they followed her back to the barn, each to its own stall. She closed them in, gave the horses their grain and the cow her hay. She milked the cow and gave the chickens their share of milk and grain. She took the rest of the milk to the house. Now she needed water for the house. Still waiting for an answer from God, she picked up the water bucket and headed back to the river. She walked along the trail, looking into the woods in the direction that her husband had gone, and hoped against hope that she would see him coming back to her. All she saw were trees. Some had lighter and some darker-colored bark. Suddenly, a gentle voice spoke to her heart. "Pull the light-colored bark from those trees; chop it up; mix it in with the grain, and feed your animals."

She stopped in her tracks. "God, I heard you! This is what Alixey has been talking about. But I am not worthy of you talking to me. I am a sinner, and You are pure," she shouted excitedly when she heard the voice. She also received joy and strength. She had no doubt that she would have strength to peel the bark from the trees.

The trek through the snow would be a challenge. There was no trail to those trees and to dig one would take a long time. Going to the trees, she would be empty-handed except for her hatchet and empty bag. But she was young and strong and confident she could do it.

After the chickens had been fed and watered, she collected a few eggs and took them into the house. She informed the girls that she was going to the woods and that they were to stay in the house with the door latched.

Anya went back to the barn, got an empty burlap bag and a hatchet and started walking toward the woods. With every step her foot cracked the icy crust, and she sank through the snow down to her knees. She was exhausted from the long difficult walk even before starting to work.

She did not feel bad about stripping the bark off the trees; after all, they would be cut down anyway and would be a part of their new home. After getting enough bark, she headed back home with half a bag. By that time her legs were cold. Snow had fallen down into her boots. The hem of her dress and the hem of her long coat had been dragging in the snow and were frozen. She had worked up a sweat and hurried home before any more of her body would get chilled. She would have to make this trip every day and was sure that after a few more trips her footprints would make some sort of a trail.

"Open the door, girls!" her voice rang out as she knocked on the door. The wind was blowing against her back, and it felt as if it were blowing down her legs into her boots. She heard Anuta unlatch the door and open it. Anya stepped inside carrying her bag of tree bark and hatchet, dropped them in front of the wood stove, took off her scarf and coat and then pulled her dress off over her head. Setting the clothes on the table, she sat in a chair and pulled off her boots, as clumps of snow fell to the floor. She took off her heavy wool socks and stood in front of the stove to warm the chill on her legs.

Swinging their legs and watching their mother, Anuta and Tanya sat on a bench near the stove. They knew she had done an arduous task and remained quiet to let her get warm.

After hanging her coat and dress on the rope behind the stove, Anya asked Anuta to get her a pair of socks from a basket under her bed. Still in her heavy linen slip, she walked over to choose a dress from where they hung on hooks along a wall. She did not have many choices. They had had to flee and had grabbed only what they could. She missed all the beautiful clothes that she had left behind, but being a gifted seamstress, she planned, once her family was all together again, to buy a new sewing machine, this time with a foot pedal instead of a hand crank. She would buy linen and make new clothes for her family and herself. Anya picked a dress with lots of buttons and put it on, along with her socks and boots.

She pulled a large wooden box out from under the kitchen counter and found her meat chopping trough. After sharpening her hatchet on a whetstone, she set the trough on the table, laid a few pieces of bark in the trough and began chopping. Slowly and patiently she kept at it.

"Is this our dinner?" Anuta asked.

"Oh, no," her mama answered with a smile. "This is dinner for the chickens and horses."

"Do they like this stuff?" Anuta asked again.

"We'll see," answered her mama, smiling.

"Why don't you keep feeding them with the grain like you have been?" Anuta asked again.

"Well, my little one, the rats have gotten into it and have eaten some of the grain. I am doing this so that we have enough to last until spring gets here with new grass."

jAnuta, now satisfied, walked to the simmering soup pot to see if breakfast was done.

"Are you girls hungry?" asked their mother. "Well, it is almost ready," she assured them as she continued to chop the pieces into the size of grain and poured them out into a bucket.

It was time to feed the horses and chickens for the evening. Anya took the chopped bark to the barn and mixed the grain in with it. The chickens went right for it, but the horses were a little slow at eating it.

This became her daily routine, and it kept the chickens and horses fed.

10

Reunion

Anya and the girls had eaten almost all the soup for lunch, leaving just enough for dinner. Soup was on their daily menu. For dessert they dipped bread into a bowl of jam, and a glass of milk helped wash it down. Some days they had cottage cheese and egg pies. No one complained. Their bellies were full, and this was a blessing for them.

After putting on her coat and scarf, Anya went out to the ice hole in the barn to get more venison for the next day. Anya opened the barn door, stepped inside and closed the door behind her. She went over to where they kept their food frozen, took a pitchfork and moved a pile of straw over to the side. Removing the boards, she could see the meat and frozen berries that she had picked during the summer. She got down on her hands and knees to choose a cut of meat, placed it in the bowl and pulled the board back over the hole. She stood up and used the pitchfork to pile the straw back over the boards to keep the ice inside the hole from thawing. Her husband would pack more snow into the ice hole at the end of winter so that it would stay frozen all through the spring, summer and fall until it could be repacked with the next winter's snow.

She bent down to pick up her bowl and heard the clang of a bell like those that are attached to a moving sleigh. *It must be Alixey!* she thought with a thrill. She rushed to the door and quickly pulled it open. Suddenly, another thought came to mind. Alixey was hiding from wolves and people; he would not be making any noise.

As she stepped out, a smile lit up her face. It was Vasili and Masha. Masha always used that same red shawl.

"Oh, my goodness!" she called out, "My dear, dear friends and neighbors from Nikolayevska!"

Vasili and Masha smiled back. Masha leapt from the moving sleigh, and they grabbed and hugged each other as Anya's wooden bowl and its contents fell to the ground. Vasili was surprised at his wife. Normally timid, this was unusual for her. He carefully brought the horses to a halt, climbed down, went over to Anya and wrapped his arms around her. Masha stepped back for a moment and then came to give Anya yet another hug.

Anya and her daughters had been living in the lonely dugout with only each other to talk to. Now they had their friends with whom to visit.

Vasili picked up the bowl and the meat and handed it back to Anya, who pointed to the house and asked them to come in. Anya had many questions to ask and much to tell.

Vasili and Masha stepped into the house and took off their heavy coats and hats. As soon as Anuta and Tanya saw them they screamed in such delight that if the house had had large windows they would have shattered. The girls jumped off their beds and ran right to their visitors. After lots of hugs and kisses everyone finally calmed down. This was the first time anyone had visited since their papa left.

Anya wanted Vasili to go over to the wash bucket since he had handled the raw meat. He walked over and took a bar of soap. Anya asked Anuta to pour water over his hands, then hers.

Even though it was after lunch, Anya asked them to have a seat at the table. She set out jam made from wild raspberries, blueberries and strawberries, all cooked together, and slices of fresh bread. She put a pot of tea on the stove to offer her welcome friends this warm delight to go with the jam and bread. She then poured everyone tea and milk, and joy filled the house.

"Tell me about your trip. And where do you live now?" Anya asked them.

"Well, the trip was uneventful. It was all blessed by God. We were able to bring quite a bit with us, even tools. We bought a dugout a little bit smaller than yours about five kilometers south of here, also on the Chubaroy River," answered Vasili.

"Do you have any close neighbors?"

"Oh, no," answered Masha. "We feel a little lonely out there."

"How did you find me?" Anya asked Vasili.

"We ran into Meernu," answered Vasili. "He said he met you on the day you arrived here, and he helped you find this place. We were in city hall to obtain our legal residency status. He stopped us to tell us about another family that moved here who was dressed the same way we were. Upon further questioning, we realized it was someone from Nikolayevska or from one of the nearby villages."

"And I'm so glad it's you," Masha interjected. "And where is your husband?"

Anya could not hide her sadness and hung her head. "We were supposed to come here with his mother and brothers, but circumstances did not allow it. The soldiers were patrolling around her home. We had to leave them, or all be caught and pay the consequences. We left with a promise that we would be back for them. Four weeks ago Alixey left on foot. He thought it would be difficult to sneak a horse in. He did take a rifle, but I hope he never had a reason to use it. I packed lots of dried bread cubes, honey, and venison jerky. He was dressed warmly; he took a fur blanket and matches. Now we sit here and wait." Anya's eyes could not hide the tears, and her face could not conceal the worry.

Masha and Vasili comforted her with the assurance that Alixey was no fool. "He will be back," Vasili said, his voice strong and reassuring. "And until he returns, Masha and I will check on you every day." Vasili looked around the three-room home. They might be a little crowded once everyone arrived. "I'll tell you what." He spoke in a sweet and gentle manner, as he usually did. "When everyone gets here, if you find there are too many of you for this home, anyone is welcome to stay with us." While Vasili was speaking, Masha sat quietly nodding her head in agreement.

Anya stood up and walked over and hugged them both. She was so grateful for such wonderful friends.

Anuta ran into the kitchen where her mother and guests were sitting, very excited. Tanya was right behind her. "Mama," she shouted, "I think I hear Papa's voice calling your name!"

Everyone fell silent to listen.

Sure enough, "Anya!" Alixey's voice called.

They all jumped to their feet, grabbed their coats and scarves and headed out the door.

Anya could not believe her eyes. It was not only her husband and his family; it was her family as well. There they were, three sleighs heading toward them.

Everyone in the sleighs was bundled up and looked cold. They were so wrapped up that she could not tell who was who.

One sleigh was being pulled by Bobka and Domka. Could that be one of her brothers and his wife driving it? And why only one brother and not the other? Did he and his wife not come along?

"Anya!" her husband called out. "I brought everyone."

Overjoyed, Anya dropped to her knees. She cupped her hands over her face as tears of joy ran down her face. Both Tanya and Anuta were jumping up and down with excitement, calling out over and over to their papa and the rest of the family.

Vasili and Masha recognized their sleigh. They had no idea that Bobka and Domka were capable of such a thing. They looked at each other in amazement and shrugged their shoulders.

"Leave it to those young men to come up with such a thing," Vasili said with a light-hearted chuckle.

"I would never be brave enough to trust those animals even if they are pets," replied Masha. She suggested to her husband, "Let's go fill the stove with more wood so everyone can warm up."

"Great idea," he replied. They headed to the large woodpile, and both of them picked up an armload and took the wood in the house. Vasili got down on his knees in front of the wood stove, opened the door and placed several pieces on the smoldering fire. Immediately the wood started to crackle.

Masha walked over to the brick oven and opened the door. It was not lit. She found some kindling and smaller pieces of wood in a box right beside the oven. She arranged them over the old ashes, and then placed bigger pieces on top. She found a match and lit the kindling. It ignited quickly, and then the smaller pieces began to crackle and burn. A sound everyone loved to hear, it meant a warm fire soon.

Masha looked around the kitchen and saw the frozen meat. This was not going to feed anyone today. "Vasili," she suggested again, "there is nothing here to feed these people. Take me back home. I have chopped and seasoned meat ready for Kutletie [meat balls]. After we get back I can make noodles, and we will feed the whole family."

He agreed, and they went outside. Vasili went to the sleigh as Masha walked over and informed Anya of her intentions.

Anya, still in tears, gave her a hug and kissed her on the cheek. "Thank you," she said to her friend.

Masha went over to the sleigh, climbed on and left with Vasili.

Trying to control her emotions, Anya watched Oseph and his father help Simon down from the sleigh. Overcome instead, she burst into loud sobbing. As the three men walked past her, she heard Simon's weak voice trying to console her.

"Oh, little sister, don't cry. I will be just fine, you will see."

Alixey quickly walked over to his sobbing wife, took her into his arms and gently pulled her close to him. "Oh, Anya, my Anya, don't cry. The worst is behind him." Alixey spoke quietly. He knew she would react this way; any caring person would.

"What happened to my brother? Is this what Stalin's army does?" she demanded.

"No, my love. He was hunting in the mountains up north and a gang of thugs shot him. When he got home, he had to be hidden. They had no time to tend to him, and as a result he lost a lot of blood and got infected. When I got there, he was already getting better. I could not leave him. If those thugs ever found him, they would kill him and his whole family.

"So, my most precious, please consider his state of mind. He has a wound in his flesh and one in his heart. Nadiya left him."

"Nadiya left him?" Anya blurted out, her voice laced with anger. "How dare she? Simon treated her like a queen, and that

77

was not good enough?" Rage filled her. She stepped away from Alixey.

"Anya, please calm down," he pleaded with her. "Be strong for your brother. He will recover. His arm will heal, and he will be the big brother that you remember him to be. But right now could you please go and tend to our company. We are all hungry, cold and tired. We only stopped long enough to rest the animals. We fought wolves in a few places. Bobka and Domka did not like the sound of the gunfire, but Oseph kept control of them. Now that we have them here, what do we do with them? Do we continue keeping them as pets, or do we let them go? But for now we will put them into the barn along with the rest of the animals. We will decide tomorrow. Right now we need to unload the sleigh. So let's go inside. I want to warm up before the men and I do this job." Alixey kissed his wife, took her hand, and both went into the crowded dwelling.

Anya took off her coat and scarf and hung them on the coat rack. Noticing that her daughters' coats were lying on the floor, she usually would have corrected the girls, but today she would excuse it. She picked them up, hung them in their places and went over to Simon, who stood up. Anya almost teared up again but held it in. After a long silent hug, she assured her big brother that he was free and would never need to look over his shoulder again.

Turning to face her long-awaited company, she informed them that Masha and Vasili would soon return with chopped meat and they would have meat balls and homemade noodles.

All were worn out from their trip. No one volunteered to help. Some sat around the table, others on the long bench along the wall, enjoying the warm air. Daved, Petro and their nieces climbed up on the brick oven. Some sat quietly while others looked around trying to make sense of this interesting residence.

They were amazed at it. How could something like this be dug into the side of a hill? Just two bedrooms, a family area and kitchen, despite all that timber growing all around.

Anya knew what they were thinking. Very little light came through the two windows. They hadn't seen a dirt floor before. The walls and ceiling consisted of boards that were painted white. She finally broke into the silence.

"This is a strange looking house, but it's very warm. We do have to use kerosene lamps during the day. The darkness made it harder when it was just the three of us. But you are all here now, and I could not be happier. Come spring, when the building and planting starts, this place will feel like the homes we had in Russia."

"Oh, my Anya," Axiniya interrupted. "Mama's big house collapsed in Nikolayevska. We think all the men that were in it were killed."

"Collapsed?" asked Anya with surprise in her voice and on her face. "That's strange. Why would it collapse?"

Alixey piped up, "I got there just in time to experience an earthquake. I was out in the barnyard when it knocked me off my feet. And that was not when the house collapsed. It was the aftershock that took it down. The ground underneath it split open and the house fell in."

"Did any other houses collapse?" Anya was very concerned for her friends.

"No," answered Alixey. "Just some windows cracked, and of course the roof slid off Mama's cabin. No one was injured. They got out when the window shattered. The roof started to crack, then slid to the ground. No one in the village knew about me being there except my family and your family. But once the roof went and all the neighbors came together to see, they saw me and were glad. I informed them where you and the girls were." Then he fell silent for a few minutes. "I have something to tell all of you. Come spring, the whole village is coming to live here. They gave me their gold to buy up as much land as I can."

Anya shrieked with joy. "That is great news. This morning I was in tears from feeling alone. Now I have all of you, and I'm so filled with joy. And you bring me this wonderful news." Her voice quavered.

"Oh, you should see all the food they sent us off with. We still have some left over," Alixey informed her.

Anya cleared the tea and jelly off the table from the afternoon's company. Placing her large bread board on the table, she filled a large bowl with flour from the barrel, went to the pantry by the front door, pulled back the curtain and took out a handful of eggs. She heaped flour on the board and made a well in it. She dipped a cup into the water bucket, filled it, poured it into the well and then cracked the eggs into it. Just before she plunged her hand into the dough, she remembered the salt. Going over to the shelf that was over the cook stove, she took a handful, walked back to the table and poured it into the waiting liquid, plunged her hand in and started mixing. Her smile was like a bright light on her face. First, she smashed the egg yolk between her fingers, then she mixed the eggs, water and salt together. Slowly she mixed all the contents to form a large dough ball. Then she kneaded it until the dough was one light yellow color. She cut the dough up into fist-sized pieces.

Her sister-in-law Zenya got up to help her. "I will roll the dough out; you go and put the water on the stove."

It was just like old times with several women working in the kitchen. Anya was getting low on water, so she started putting on her coat and scarf. Alixey knew what she needed. He jumped up to go get it for her.

"Oh, no, Alixey. You rest. I will take care of this." She took two buckets and a yoke, quickly stepped outside and closed the door behind her as everyone watched her leave.

Anya felt so light. The heaviness was gone. Her whole family was under one roof. What more could she ask for? She thought of doing a little dance but decided against it. What if she slipped and fell or someone saw her? Instead, she quietly sang a song as she walked.

As she approached the watering hole, she could see a thin sheet of ice over it. She smashed the ice with the bottom of the bucket, and it shattered and disappeared into the flowing current. She bent down, dipped one bucket in the water and filled it, then the other. She set them down side by side; then, lifting the handle of one bucket, she hooked one end of the yoke to it. Moving the other bucket to approximately the right distance, she hooked the other end of the yoke to the other handle. She squatted down and placed the yoke across the back of her neck. As she stood up, the buckets were lifted up with the yoke now resting comfortably across her shoulders. Trying hard not to splash, she started back. This was not a burdensome task for her; she did it several times a day.

When she got to the front door, her husband pulled it open and took the buckets. "Now listen to me. From now on, Daved and Petro will fetch the water. You will be too busy with all the things that need to be done around here." He leaned over and kissed her cheek.

"As you wish," she remarked with a smile.

Zenya had rolled out a few balls of dough, with several left to do.

Suddenly there was a knock at the door. Daved jumped down from the brick oven and opened the door to find Vasili and Masha carrying something wrapped in dish towels. Masha had a large bowl of chopped meat, and Vasili had a bowl of vegetables to be chopped up and cooked into a sauce for the noodles and meat balls.

Anya cleared a place on the counter and they laid their loads down. She took out a large cooking pot and two cast iron skillets from a box between the brick oven and the wall.

Fedosia, who had been quiet until now, stood up and told Vasili that she would take over. She peeled and cut up all the vegetables. Remembering the pickled tomatoes, she asked Oseph to go bring them in. They would be really good in this sauce.

Oseph stood up and took his coat and hat while Alixey, Daved and Petro did the same. It was time to unload the sleigh and put the animals into the barn.

Alixey suggested that they unload the groceries in the barn.

Anya remembered about the rats. "Oh, no, not in the barn," she told them. "We have rats."

Daved smiled. "Rats," he said. "I love to hunt rats. Tomorrow I will fix a trap they will not be able to resist."

Petro nodded his head and laughed out loud.

"What is so funny?" Anya asked.

"Well, it is a good thing you don't have cats. They like the traps too."

Axiniya smiled and told everyone how their cat almost drowned in the trap he once set up. Everyone had a good chuckle. They were all in such great spirits. They were all together, and the place where they were was warm and safe. There were no usurpers around, no one to fear. The future looked promising.

The sleighs were unloaded and all the foodstuffs were packed into the pantry. The bedding was stacked anywhere there was room. The animals, including the reindeer, were put in the barn.

Dinner smelled wonderful. There wasn't enough room for everyone at the table, so some held their plates in their laps while they ate. Afterward the women collected the dishes and utensils and washed them in a bucket of warm water that was waiting on the stove.

Vasili stood up and announced to everyone that they had a room in their house and that whoever wanted to go with them was welcome to stay there until their new homes were ready.

Feodor and Fedosia talked quietly between themselves for a few minutes, and then announced that their family would go with them.

Anya stood up quickly and said, "Simon stays here with us. The girls will keep him company. In fact, he can have their bed. You know it would be difficult for him to get in and out of the sleigh to come here and leave." She said this with such force that no one dared to disagree with her.

Those who were leaving again hitched the horses to the sleigh, packed their bedding and went with the kind neighbors.

Throughout the winter, everyone visited with one another. Daved and his clever rat trap got rid of all the rats. Alixey and his brothers continued to peel the tree bark and mix it in with the grain to feed their horses and chickens. Domka and Bobka liked the bark all by itself.

Eventually they all went to the city and became legal aliens. Now they had permission to be there. Alixey bought all the land he could along the Chubaroy River, more than enough for all of them and their grazing animals. The officials were happy with them—the area was no longer deemed wilderness; it would finally be populated with animals and agriculture—so they gave them additional land to keep and with which they could do whatever they wanted.

11

Spring at Last

Winter was coming to an end. Patches of green grass could be seen here and there. The river, no longer iced over, rose. The girls were instructed to stay away from it lest they be swept away in the rapid current.

Every morning after the chores were done and breakfast was served, the men went to the forest to cut down trees. After the trees were felled, they were stripped of bark and the branches were cut and smoothed off.

Clay was needed to fill in the seams between logs. The women were assigned to ride around the soft hills and the countryside looking for a bare hillside or one with very little green on it. This meant dense ground with clay, just what they needed.

Anya and her sister-in-law Zenya saddled up and headed east. They were impressed with the terrain and the delicate snow flowers. This area had far more beauty than where they came from, even though the trees were still bare. The women were so excited that the trees would soon put out their green leaves. Pussy willows ornamented the branches of some of the bushes. The air was so much warmer that there was no longer a need for a scarf or a long coat; just a jacket was enough. They saw birds, absent during the winter, perched on the branches and chirping as if cheering them on.

Anya felt as if she could ride all day and look at the scenery. But they were on a mission, and so far no clay. Perhaps it was hidden under a patch of snow. Both women decided to turn back and head for home. No longer looking around, they just visited. Zenya had something to tell her sister-in-law; she was going to have a baby.

Anya had become suspicious when Zenya had started to complain of how bad eggs smelled.

"Does Oseph know?" she asked, pleased.

"No, I haven't said anything yet. We are a little crowded in Vasili and Masha's home already. And I'm worried that Masha may be a little envious. She wants children but doesn't have any yet."

"No, don't worry about that. Masha will be glad to have a baby around. She loves them. They've only been married two years. I haven't put her on the barren list yet."

Suddenly, Anya's horse's hoof seemed to stick to something it stepped in. Anya was jolted forward and almost flew headlong off the horse. She reined in the horse and dismounted, afraid that it had injured its leg. Going around to the horse's head, her foot also stuck in the same ground. She pulled to free herself and her foot came out of the boot. Standing on one foot, she held on to the horse with one hand and pulled her boot free with the other. She hopped away from the mud on one foot and pulled her boot back on. Returning to the mud, she tried to pick some up with her hand. It was dense, and no grass grew on it.

"Clay," she called out. "We have found clay. Hallelujah!" She needed to hang something on a bush nearby to mark the area so she could find it again. Perhaps she had a handkerchief? She searched her pockets. Nothing, she had nothing in her pockets.

Zenya searched her own pockets. She had nothing either.

"Well, we need something." She reached under her dress, pulled down her bloomers and tied them onto the bush, intending to come back with a handkerchief and to reclaim her bloomers before she was found out.

Zenya was sitting up on her horse laughing so hard that tears ran down her cheeks.

"Don't tell anyone," Anya instructed her sister-in-law.

Zenya assured her she was safe.

Anya was not happy with the draft that she felt when she remounted her horse. "I am coming back here with something else to mark this bush and taking back my bloomers." She started laughing herself.

"I will come back with you. I want to keep you company," Zenya told her.

After Anya's bloomers were reclaimed and the bush was marked, they rode on, bringing a hot lunch to where their husbands were working. Zenya sat down on a log by her husband. He peeled an egg, took a bite and then handed her the rest as a love gesture. She smelled the egg, jumped to her feet, then ran and vomited behind a tree.

Alixey clapped his hands together and laughed.

"What is so funny?" Oseph asked, offended at him.

"Oseph, don't you know what's happening here?" he asked.

"My wife is not feeling well. That's what's happening." His answer was full of offense.

Anya was sitting next to Alixey in silence. This was not a conversation in which she dared to get involved. Zenya needed to talk to her husband. She gently pressed her elbow into her husband's side. Right away he knew that Oseph was clueless, so he apologized to his brother-in-law and assured him that she would be better soon. They quickly changed the subject while they continued with their meal.

"Are you all right?" Oseph called out to his wife.

"Are you done eating eggs?" she called back.

"I can be," he answered, still completely mystified.

Daved and Petro did not know what was happening, so they just kept silent and took advantage of the rest and of the delicious meal.

Vasili had seen this with his older sister, so he too knew what was happening. But after seeing what passed between the two men, he had the right to remain silent, and he was.

By the end of the day, the men had felled several trees. They collected their double-handed saws, axes, hatchets and planes and headed home, ready for a hot meal and a soft bed.

After the houses were built, the men got together and built a bath house next to the river. The bath house was a rough square building with two rooms. The outer room had benches and was used as a dressing area, while the inner room had two decks, upper and lower, built of smooth sawn logs purchased from a distant town. A huge tub, around and in which rocks were piled high, sat on a cast iron wood stove in the inner room.

It was Saturday. Before the meal, the men had first to go take the steam baths that their wives had prepared for them. They would then eat while the women and the two girls bathed. All the men walked into the dressing area and set their clean clothes on the benches that were along two walls while Feodor lit the lantern as they all undressed. They filed into the inner room and closed the door behind them. The lantern there was also lit, and the air was hot and dry. The stove had had three loads of wood burned in it, and the rocks on it were now very hot. A large wash tub was also heating on the stove. Another tub, this one with cold water, sat on the floor.

Daved filled a ladle with cold water and threw it onto the rocks. Steam filled the room, making the air easier to breathe. Alixey took an empty basin and ladled hot water into it, then added cold. It was a little too hot, so he added more cold water. When it was just right, he poured some on his head. Taking a bar of soap, he lathered and scrubbed his hair and face, then his beard. He rinsed it all off and climbed up on the upper deck to sweat. While he sat there, the others took turns washing their hair, faces and beards, and joined him. Once in a while someone would throw more cold water on the hot rocks. The steam would fill the room, especially the upper deck.

One by one the men got too hot and came back down to the lower deck. After washing and rinsing off the soap, they went out and got dressed. Before leaving, Oseph refilled the stove with a load of wood so that the women would have enough heat.

All the men were invited to Anya and Alixey's for dinner, where the women had prepared a huge venison roast with baked potatoes, steamed carrots and nice warm bread. And, of course, wild berry jam for dipping the bread and herb tea for washing it all down. The men walked in and were greeted by the women. The food was on the table. The house was warm and welcoming. The men dished up, found a place to sit and relaxed while they ate.

The women and the two young ladies left to take their turn in the bath house. When they returned, it was their turn to eat. Afterwards they cleaned up and washed the dishes. After a lengthy visit the guests left.

Zenya was ready to tell her husband why the eggs were making her sick. That night no one could have seen a happier man. He dropped to his knees, kissed Zenya's stomach and wrapped his arms around her hips while keeping his cheek up against her stomach as if he were listening to this brand new life. Zenya lost count of how many times he thanked her.

Finally he stood up, took both of her hands in his, looked straight into her eyes and made her a promise that he would be a very attentive father and provide for both their needs. He assured her she had nothing to worry about and asked her to take care of herself and this new life that was growing in her. He could not wait to share the news with the rest of her family although some of them already suspected, and others knew.

12
Hope

Simon was completely recovered from the bullet wound. Free of the sling, he had full use of his left arm. His strength had returned. He felt completely whole in his flesh, but there was still a hole in his heart for Nadiya. He wished that someday he could contact her to see if she were doing all right. It grieved him to think she was so unhappy; it wasn't always that way. He could remember happier times, but for some unknown reason she had become silent and distant. Was it his fault? Was it something he did? Their marriage had been arranged, as most marriages were, by both of their parents, but he loved her and was very happy with their choice. He was sure she had felt the same way about him, but something had changed. No one but Anya knew how deep this private pain of his ran. He could not fool her; she saw how he looked at her girls. He too wanted to be a good spouse and father. He involved himself in all the family activities and worked along with his brother and father and all the other men, but eventually he had begun to feel like a robot. He had his daily routine down to the very last detail and did it well, but inside he felt hollow; nothing else could take her place. His only comfort was knowing that their church would not allow her to remarry.

Divorce was only allowed in cases of physical abuse or infidelity, and there was none of that. He hoped that eventually she would get lonely and come to him. When his father wrote his sisters of their destination, he requested that they contact her and invite her to come to them. Oh, how he waited and longed for that day!

It wasn't long before people started showing up from Nikolayevska. Some days it was just one wagon, on others a wagon train. They were all in one accord about who got what area of land. The homes were to be built along the river. The horses were hobbled and set loose in the pastures. Pythons, cobras, and other venomous snakes were sometimes seen in that area, but they stayed away from horses. Gradually more houses were built. With the help of friends and relatives, Alixey built a large house for his family, one for Vasili and Masha, then one for Feodor and Fedosia. Oseph and Zenya moved in with them since families lived together. They had a beautiful little girl and named her Zina. Simon continued to live with Alixey and Anya in their spacious home.

Anya was now expecting a third child. Alixey's mother Axiniya, Daved and Petro had a home built between Alixey's and Feodor's homes. Each had a large lot.

Once again Alixey built himself a grain mill. Everyone planted wheat fields, potatoes and vegetable gardens. Their barnyards once again teemed with cows, chickens, geese and ducks. There were clusters of beehives along the hillsides. Once again there was harmony, prosperity and peace in this village like in the one they had left behind.

More earthquakes followed in Nikolayevska. Stalin lost interest in that area. He deemed it uninhabitable and evacuated all his troops. By that time most of their neighbors and friends had left the village. There was no one to fear. So Yakov and Samsun took apart the sawmill, packed up all the metal parts and components and casually left for China. Their new sawmill was in constant production. Everyone wanted cut planks for their floors and barns and chicken coops.

Everyone got together and hashed around names for the new village. First they thought to name it after Alixey and his family, but Alixey did not want that and said the village should be named after the river since they had settled there because of it. He reminded them of all the fish that had been caught in it and that they were eating. So the village was called Chubaroyka and was even registered in the city hall under that name.

One morning Anuta was hanging out the wash on the line when she heard a cat meow. This was strange—no one brought cats along—so she ignored it. Then she heard two cats meow and this piqued her interest. It sounded a lot like Murka and Kiska. She left the wash and headed in the direction of the sounds. The grass was tall, and hard to see into. She decided to step out in faith and called for the cats. "Murka! Kiska!" Right away she heard them meowing back to her. She could see movement in the grass. Her heart was racing, overjoyed, but she feared it might not be them at all.

Suddenly a white fluffy head appeared out of the grass, then the rest of the long white-haired creature stood in front of her. Right behind her was an orange tabby. It was Murka and Kiska! She scooped them up and ran to the house to surprise her sister.

"Tanya! Tanya!" she called out. "The cats are here!"

Anya was in the kitchen but went into the family room where she heard Anuta's voice chuckling and calling for her sister. Anya stood amazed, looking at the two animals. "Wow!" was all that she could say as she stood there looking at her daughter holding both cats, who looked too worn out to protest about how they were being held.

Tanya raced down the stairs squealing with joy. "Kiska, Murka, you are here!" She ran up to her sister and took Murka, her favorite. She had always loved that yellow cat more than Kiska. Tanya was Murka's favorite also. In Russia they had been inseparable. Now they were together again.

Anya stood and watched her girls hugging and loving them. She had heard of something called a camera, and at that moment she wished she had one. It gave her so much joy to see her girls so happy and laughing so gaily.

Anuta looked over at her mama and in a giddy voice she asked, "Mama, how did they find us? This place is so far away!"

"Love always finds a way," Anya answered. "Girls, take the cats to the barn and take a bowl of milk with you. They need to learn that the barn is the place they will be fed. Then go wash your hands and finish your chores. Let the cats get some rest; they will come to see you after that."

Anuta and Tanya took the bowl of milk their mama gave them. Anuta carried the milk, Tanya took the cats, and they headed for the barn.

Anya felt so full of love and joy. She remembered what life was like a year before. The fear. The emptiness. The loneliness. She murmured, "God, you are God of all. You are God when we are full of sorrow and you are God when we are full of joy. You never stop being our God. Thank you for guiding those cats to us. When we think something's impossible, You make it possible. Would you guide Nadiya back to Simon? He is broken without her. Thank you for being our God. Amen."

She hoped this was true, but in her reasoning mind she knew it was impossible. The cats showed up because they loved the girls enough to try. But she did not think Nadiya loved Simon enough to think of him, let alone travel this far. She decided to stop dwelling on that and returned to getting supper ready. She could not afford to get upset. She was pregnant and when she got riled, her baby did not move around like it should. It was as if Baby knew that Mama was unhappy. Besides, it was due soon.

Alixey opened the door and called out, "Anya, come quick! I have news."

She set the mixing spoon down and slowly walked to the door. Her husband had been working out in the barn and was covered with wood chips and dust. He did not want to track any into the house.

He took her hand as she went over to him and smiled. In a gentle voice, he began to speak. "A family from Nadiya's village just got here. They're also having trouble with Stalin's troops. And," he continued, "it seems Nadiya was pregnant when she left. She did not know it at the time. She had a son. Now she wants to know, if she moves down here, can she stay with us if Simon does not take her back."

Anya almost lost her balance when she heard the news. "Oh, of course Simon will take her back," she answered. She could not be happier. God was God of all. She could not wait to tell Simon but decided against it. What if Nadiya changed her mind and decided not to come? It would mean more suffering that he would have to endure.

"There is more news," Alixey added. "Nikolayevska is a lake now. There was another great quake, felt in other villages. Water started flowing up from the place where Mama's house used to be. There is no sign of even one house."

Anya heard him talk about the house and the lake, but her mind was still on the previous news. "Let's not say anything to Simon. We will surprise him," she blurted out.

Alixey wondered why they should surprise him with the news of the village being a lake.

Anya realized his conversation had moved on to the village, and she was still thinking about Nadiya and her son. "No, no, let's not tell him about Nadiya or their son. You know he will be so anxious to see her. He will worry himself sick waiting for her."

This made sense to Alixey. "You're right. I'd better go talk to those people and ask them not to say anything and explain why."

"Thank you, Alixey. I'd better get back to the kitchen or we'll have a burned dinner." She reached out and gave her husband a hug and returned to the hot kitchen. The thought of Simon and his Nadiya back together became so real to her. God answered her prayer while still in her heart, even before she put it into words. She teared up and started thanking Him.

Simon had been doing some work over at his parents'. He walked into the house just in time to overhear his sister tearfully thanking God. He smiled, walked over to her and gave her a hug and a kiss on the cheek. He pulled away from her, looked down into those beautiful brown eyes and agreed with the fact that she had a lot to be thankful for.

"Oh, Simon," she thought, "if you only knew."

"Yes, I do have a lot to be thankful for. I have my whole family, wonderful parents, a priceless mother-in-law, Alixey and his brothers, my two daughters and now my new child, our beautiful homes and this village. Everything is perfect, my wonderful brother. Now go wash up for dinner. It's almost ready. Could you please go get Anuta and Tanya? They are in the barn. Murka and Kiska showed up a little while ago."

Simon flinched as if someone had flicked him on the forehead. "Are you talking about the cats?" he asked in a high-pitched voice.

"Yes, I was very surprised, shocked, actually. How is it that some predator did not get them? And how did they know which direction to travel in?"

"I don't know," answered Simon, "but I am so glad for those girls. At least now they will leave the chickens alone."

"Chickens? What have they been doing to the chickens?"

"Oh, they've been wrapping them up like babies in old rags and carrying them around. Tanya even put a diaper on one of your red hens. Now when she sees Tanya, she runs and hides."

"Well, that explains why they haven't been laying eggs like I thought they should. I was starting to worry that perhaps we were sold older chickens. Well, it is a good thing the cats are finally here," Anya continued with her hands on her hips. The hands on the hips were not so much for the gesture as for the slight labor pains that she had started feeling during the conversation.

"All right, I will go get the girls," Simon told his sister as he was about to leave.

"Well, listen Simon, you know what? I would prefer that you find my husband first."

Simon was totally oblivious to what was going on as he went to find his brother-in-law.

When Simon found Alixey, walking home from a neighbors' house, he told him that Anya wanted him home for dinner. This was not her normal routine; they waited until he got home before the table was set. He knew this meant, "Come home now," so he quickened his pace, knowing it must have something to do with the baby. Before he walked into the house, he quickly brushed himself off so he would not bring any debris into the house. He walked in, and there was water on the floor where she had been standing.

She was in pain and was leaning against the banister. She asked him to go get the midwife.

Alixey went straight to the corral and called two of his horses, one for himself and the other for the midwife.

Simon, in the barn with the girls, was taking a turn petting the cats when he heard his brother-in-law calling the horses. He knew it had something to do with the baby. He went over to him and asked, "Alixey, what's going on?"

"It's Anya," Alixey answered. "She's in labor. Will you please take the girls to Mama's for the night? I need to go get the midwife."

"Yes, not a problem. But first let me help you saddle the horses."

Alixey rode out, holding the reins of the extra horse.

Simon told the girls that they needed to show the cats to their grandmother Axiniya and their uncles and that they could spend the night over at their grandmother's.

They were excited. They headed toward the house to ask their parents if it were all right with them if they did that, but Simon stopped them and assured them it was their idea. Tanya and Anuta swooped up the cats to go show them off to their grandmother.

When Simon walked in and announced to Axiniya that the girls were there to spend the night with the cats, she knew immediately what was going on. She set three more places on the table. After dinner, Daved and Petro invited Simon and the girls to go fishing on the river.

The next morning while Axiniya was frying the freshly caught fish, Alixey walked in and told them he had seen them at the river the evening before.

"Were you fishing last night too, Papa?" Anuta asked.

"No, my little one, I went to fetch a bucket of water for your mama, and there was a little baby girl just floating on top of the current. I quickly waded in and scooped her up in the bucket and brought her home. So now you have a little sister. But you had better let your mama take care of her, and you can be little mothers to the cats. All right?" he asked.

By now the girls were so excited they started looking for their shoes. They wanted to go home and meet their little sister.

"Oh, no, my little ones, not without your breakfast," their grandmother Axiniya told them. She had made them a pot of porridge from crushed wheat and milk. "Now everyone, find a seat at the table and let's eat." She gave the girls porridge, and the adults ate the fish.

Anuta and Tanya ran into the house expecting their mama to greet them at the door with the new family member. But she wasn't there.

"Where is Mama?" Anuta asked her father.

"She is upstairs in bed resting. You can go up quietly, but don't wake Feta," whispered their father.

"Who is Feta?" asked Tanya.

"She is your sister."

The girls quietly walked up the stairs and into their parents' bedroom. Grandmama Fedosia and Aunt Zenya were there. They had brought food for the mother. Feta was a tiny little thing, so tiny that the girls were afraid to touch her, fearing she might break. Adoringly they looked at her and decided to leave the handling to their mother.

"Well, what do you think girls? Shall we keep her?" Anya quietly asked.

"Oh, yeah, Mama," answered Tanya. "Anuta and I have Murka and Kiska, and you have Feta."

Their mother gave a weak chuckle and said just above a whisper, "All right, we have a deal."

"All right, girls, let's go downstairs and leave Mama and Feta alone," their father whispered. "Let's not wake the new family member."

Simon appeared in the doorway. "Is this my new little niece?" he whispered.

"Yes, it is," answered Anya. She was very tired and hoped for the return of her strength. She was not one to lie around. She wanted to be up and around when Simon's wife arrived.

13

Nadiya

Two weeks later Anya was back to her old self. Feta had filled out a little and was becoming a little lady. She was so dainty and her cry so feminine. Anuta and Tanya both had loud booming voices. When they cried, the neighbors heard them. Now here was this new life from the same parents and yet so different. Anya knew Feta would demand more attention, but she did not mind. She fed her little one and laid her down for a nap in the crib in the family room. She needed to go and wash out a load of diapers. This would be a daily ritual for a long time, but it was worth it.

All of a sudden Anuta came bursting through the door, panting, quite out of breath. "Mama, come quick, there are three wagons coming this way, come and see!"

"Quiet," Anya whispered. "Feta just went down for a nap."

This time Anuta whispered it. "Mama, come quick! There are three wagons coming this way, come and see."

Anya chuckled. "All right, let's go see, my sweet."

Anuta led, and her mother followed. They walked out to the edge of their yard to see if it was anyone they knew or if someone needed lodging for a few days.

Anya could see three wagons, too far away to make out faces. She hoped one was bringing her sister-in-law. It was hard to be patient. But she had no choice, so she stood and just waited.

Swaying back and forth with their heavy loads, the wagons slowly approached. Finally the first wagon was close enough, but she did not recognize anyone.

Anuta started waving at someone.

"Who are you waving at?" her mother asked.

"Look, it's Aunt Nadiya," she answered.

"In which wagon?"

"Not the one in front but the one after," Anuta answered and pointed.

Anya focused on that second wagon, and it did look like her, ut she wasn't holding a child. Where was he? *Maybe it wasn't she after all,* she thought to herself. As the wagon got closer, Anya was sure that it was indeed Nadiya. She recognized that round beautiful face. Tears of joy flowed down her cheeks as she felt her anxiety melt away.

"Where is your papa and Uncle Simon?" she asked Anuta.

"They took Domka and Bobka to Meernu. He came by earlier today. He wanted to buy them. But they were gone. They have been jumping the corral fence. When they came home, they were caught and taken over there."

"Well, they will be better served over there, I suppose. They have nothing to do around here. Run next door and get your uncles Daved and Petro, hurry!"

Anuta turned and ran toward her uncle's house.

Anya wiped her tears and waited for Nadiya's wagon to come to a stop. When it finally did, Anya walked over and waited for Nadiya to get down. Anya did not recognize the driver of the wagon; she politely greeted him, and then turned her attention to her sister-in-law. "Welcome, my dear. It is so wonderful to finally have you join us."

Nadiya returned Anya's greeting. She had worried that she might not be received. "I missed all of you, and I hope I am welcome."

"You are very welcome and needed," Anya replied.

Nadiya introduced the driver to her sister-in-law. "Anya, this is my brother-in-law Foma. My sister died in childbirth two months ago, so he decided to move to Kalgatone, a village south of here. He gave me a ride.

"I am very sorry for your loss, sir," Anya said to him. "Where is your child?" she asked.

"He became ill two weeks later and died," Foma told her.

"Oh, I'm so sorry to hear that. There are no words for that kind of pain. Nevertheless I wish I could be of some comfort. May God help you to get through this.

"I would like to thank you for bringing my sister-in-law back to us," Anya continued.

"You are very welcome." He jumped off the wagon and came around to help Nadiya down.

Once her feet were on the ground, Anya went over and gave her a warm welcoming hug. "You are needed around here. Simon does not know you are coming. We didn't tell him; we wanted to surprise him. He will be very, very glad to have you back," Anya whispered in her ear.

Nadiya pulled back a little. "Well, I am not alone. There is a little man sleeping in his crib in the wagon. His name is Leonid."

"Oh, my goodness, a little one," Anya said through a smile, "Leonid was Simon's favorite uncle's name."

"I know that, that is why I gave it to him. Before we continue, I need to ask your forgiveness. I know I did a terrible thing to you and your family. You see, I was hurt over something that was said, supposedly by Simon. But I found out later that Simon never said it."

"What was said?"

"A young lady told me that Simon referred to me as the barren one. That made me so ashamed and angry. I confronted him, and he denied even thinking it. That same woman later came back to me after Simon had left. She told me she had fabricated that lie because she wanted Simon for herself. She wanted to split us up. She came to me disguised as a concerned friend and fed me a lie that destroyed our marriage. I was pregnant and didn't know it when I left.

"Do you think Simon will take me back?"

"Oh, yes, he will," Anya blurted. "You were victims of a rumor, but now it's over. Simon is staying with us, and so are you. He will be back soon. Get Leonid and come on in; you must be hungry and tired. The men will soon unload your things and bring them in."

Daved and Petro came out of their house followed by their mother. They each greeted Nadiya with warmth and kindness. They invited her to visit any time.

Leonid heard the noise and realized the wagon wasn't rocking anymore. He started crying. Axiniya, Daved and Petro stood around him, cooing.

Daved climbed up into the wagon, lifted the little crib and handed it down to his brother.

Anya led, and Nadiya followed with Petro carrying the crib behind them. When they walked into the house, little Feta was awakened by the noise and started to cry.

"You have a baby in this house?" Nadiya asked.

"Yes, she's two weeks old. Her name is Feta."

They walked up to Feta's crib and Petro set down Leonid's crib next to his cousin's. Now both babies were crying. Their mothers picked them up, and Anya invited Nadiya to have a seat at the dining room table. Carrying Feta in one arm, she set the table with the other. She dished up a bowl of stew and sliced some bread that had been baked earlier that morning.

Anya's mother-in-law came in and took Feta from her so that she could be a good hostess to her sister-in-law. Anya sat down with her and poured each of them a cup of herb tea so that they could visit while Nadiya ate.

Petro and Daved started carrying Nadiya's luggage into the front room and left it there in a pile. When they were finished, Axiniya motioned Daved to come over and handed Feta to him and told him to take care of her. She told Petro to take care of Leonid, so his mother could eat. She said she was going home to get something that she had baked earlier that morning and left.

Anya heard the voices of her parents outside. They were welcome. Her father pushed the door open and called out, "May we enter?"

"Come on in," she called out to them.

They came into the house and Nadiya hurried over to them. Feodor and Fedosia both gave her a welcoming hug.

"How are you, my dear?" Fedosia asked.

Nadiya looked down at the floor for a few seconds then cleared her throat. She needed their forgiveness and did not know how to start.

Feodor spoke first. "Welcome home. We are glad you finally came back to us. You were missed and needed."

Tears were now running down Nadiya's cheeks. "I am so sorry for the pain I caused everyone—would you please forgive me?"

"Well, first, we were never upset with you. We were worried about you," Feodor told her.

"I was unhappy, but now that has been resolved," Nadiya answered. That out of the way, she said, "Please come and meet your grandson, Leonid." She led them to where Petro sat holding him.

Feodor and Fedosia could hardly contain themselves. The young man looked just like his father. While they were doting over the child, Nadiya excused herself and went to the kitchen to ask Anya where the outhouse was. Anya walked her to the back door, opened it and pointed.

No sooner had Nadiya gone out the back door than Simon came in through the front. Seeing the pile of luggage, he asked who was moving. He turned and looked at it again to make sure it wasn't his.

"No one is moving out," his mother answered as she walked into the front room carrying little Leonid.

Simon looked at him and felt a special bond to him. "Whose child is this?" he asked.

"This is your son, Leonid," his mother answered. "And the luggage belongs to Nadiya. She has come to be your wife again."

Not believing any of what he was being told, he chuckled. "Oh, Mama, why would you tease me like that?"

Anya walked into the room with a somber look and quickly interjected, "Simon, she had sent a message that she was coming with your son. We kept it from you just in case she decided against it, so you would be spared more heartache. This is your son, and this is her luggage. She is outside and will be back shortly."

"Mama, Papa, let's go into the kitchen and leave them alone." They heard her at the back door washing her hands. Fedosia handed Leonid to Simon and left.

The back door opened. Simon's heart started leaping for joy. He heard her step inside and the clomp, clomp of her shoes as she walked across the floor. Simon stood stock still. Now he knew it was all true. This was his son, and his wife was about to enter the room.

"Hello, Simon, did you meet your son?" she stuttered.

Without another word, he took one giant step toward her and grabbed her and held her tight. Speechless, he buried his face in her hair and just held her and his son.

"I am so sorry for the pain I have caused you," she whispered.

"No, no, I am the one to blame. I failed you. Otherwise you would not have left," Simon replied.

"Listen to me, Simon. I was a fool. I listened to a lie and believed it. I let it become a wedge between us."

"What lie?" he asked.

"The lie about you referring to me as your barren wife. I felt such shame, and when Anya and Alixey had Tanya, I snapped inside. But when the one who started the lie came to me and confessed the truth, you were already gone, and I realized I was pregnant."

Simon hugged her even tighter. He started to sob. "And I was not there for you at the time you needed me. Please forgive me. What we need to do is to forgive each other." He pulled back. His eyes were wet with tears of joy. He looked into her eyes, asked her again for forgiveness and forgave her. She laid her head on his chest and started weeping while he held her and their son. In one moment he had been reunited with the love of his life. No longer a hollow empty man, he was a husband and father. "What more can I ask for?" he said quietly.

Daved heard him. "Well, you could ask me and Petro to carry your luggage up to your room."

Simon burst out in laughter. "All right. Daved and Petro, could you please carry Nadiya's luggage up to my room?"

"We would love to," Daved replied.

Axiniya pushed the door open and called out, "May we enter?"

"Please come in," Anya called back.

Axiniya had a large bowl of food. In it were savory and sweet pastries. She walked into the kitchen and set it on the table.

"Mama," Anya called to her, "would you please be the hostess? I need to go wash out a load of diapers." Then she turned to her own mother. "Mama, could you please keep an eye on Feta? I will be back soon." She headed out the door and took the tub and a bar of soap along with some diapers. Before heading to the river, she peeked into the barn to see where her daughters were. They were up in the hayloft. She could not see them, but she could hear them.

"Anuta, Tanya, are you up there alone?" she called out to them.

"We are up here with the cats," answered Anuta.

"And one chicken," added Tanya.

"I'm going to the river. I will be back soon," she called back to them.

Anya hurried toward the river to finish her chore. She knew that more visitors would be dropping by. Soon news would spread throughout the whole village. Simon was well liked and people were going to drop in to welcome Nadiya home.

Alixey was at the river to check on the fish basket that he had placed there. When he pulled it up, he found several fish. Anya saw him and called out to him. Picking up the basket with fish in it, he went over to her and gave her a hug and kiss.

"So... Simon's wife is back I hear. That is good news. Listen, my sweet, you have enough to do. I will milk the cows and have the girls collect the eggs." Holding the basket up, he added, "And then we are eating fresh fish."

"I will fry the fish," Anya told him, "but first you clean it. Oh, by the way, we have a houseful," she informed him.

"Oh, good, I love company." Giving her one more kiss, he headed home with his fish.

Anuta

14

Growth

As time went on Simon and Nadiya bought some land not too far from their family. All the men from the village gathered and helped them build a big beautiful home. They lived happy lives together, having had more children, two girls and one more boy.

Alixey and Anya also had more children. They had Natasha, Lara, Mark and Katiya, six daughters and one son. Natasha was as sweet as a summer's gentle breeze and looked just like her two oldest sisters. Lara was just like Feta, very ladylike and looked very much like Feta only with a little bit of a temper. Mark was in every way like his father, gentle and soft spoken. His topaz blue eyes could bring calm to any tormented soul. Katiya was in every way like her mother, but she had a little bit of a wild oat in her. Her parents were sure that she would grow out of it like her two older sisters.

It was a happy home. Anya had fewer chores to do. She just delegated them to the girls.

Alixey kept busy working at the grain mill and did very well for himself.

Daved and Petro got older and met and married young ladies, but continued to live in the same home with their mother, now old and failing.

Masha referred to herself as "the barren one" until she discovered she was pregnant and gave birth to twins. Due to the difficult delivery she couldn't get pregnant again, but she and Vasili were happy with the two boys and named them Daved and Petro after Alixey's inseparable brothers.

Oseph and Zenya had three more children, Georgiy, Leonid and Sasha.

Anuta was now fourteen, and a young man named Daniel caught her eye. He was a soft-spoken gentle man with deep blue eyes and brown hair, tall and muscular. She hoped he would someday notice her as well, but she told no one, not even Tanya. The girls were inseparable and withheld nothing from each other, so Anuta felt bad that she was keeping this from Tanya, but she could not risk the secret slipping out or the response of her parents. What if it were to get back to Daniel? She would be humiliated, and he might start to avoid her.

She did not know that she had already caught Daniel's interest and that he was trying to build up the courage to talk to her about how he felt.

One day Anuta got on her horse and went off into the hills to pick wild raspberries. She loved the way they smelled, and how the tall grass swayed in the gentle early summer breeze. The birds were chirping, the butterflies were fluttering from bush to bush. This peace and quiet she never got at home except at night.

Daniel was out looking for a horse that the evening before had gotten free from its hobble. He had tracked it to the same area where Anuta was picking her berries. When he saw her picking and heard her humming to herself, he decided to go over to visit her.

She was so focused that she did not hear him ride up. "Well, hello there, beautiful," he said. His voice disturbed her reverie and she started. Recognizing the voice, she quickly turned in his direction and almost knocked over the bucket of berries.

"Oh, you startled me," she squealed. But what she really meant was, I am so glad it's you.

He climbed off his horse, came over to her and started to help her pick. "So, how long have you been here?" he asked.

"Well, this bucket was empty when I got here. Now it's half full. That's how long I've been here," she said with a saucy smile. "And what are you doing here?"

"My father's horse wandered off during the night. I have tracked him to this area," he answered, his eyes fixed on Anuta. "But I am so glad I found you here."

"Well, I am not lost."

"Oh, but I am."

"What do you mean you're lost? The village is just south of us."

Daniel's voice softened. Taking his eyes off her, he blurted it out. "I am lost without you. I have deep feelings for you. I know we are young, but I do not want anyone else but you. Please don't be frightened. I am not here to harm you. I have been carrying these feelings for a while, and I am hoping that some day you will feel the same way."

A transparent person who could never hide anything, Anuta's first thought was, *This is too easy*. Embarrassed and overwhelmed by his response, she flushed and fumbled to express the deep emotions that flooded her. She decided just to be forthright as usual. "All right," she responded. "I accept your feelings and I return the same feelings to you."

Daniel blinked as if a gust of wind had hit him in the face.

He gently took Anuta into his arms and kissed her cheek, and then he whispered into her ear, "I love you."

"I love you, too," Anuta responded quietly.

Daniel let go of her, stepped back and asked her to keep this conversation just between them for now for her sake, to protect her from any gossip. He also wanted to talk to her father and get permission to visit her in the evenings.

Mutely she nodded her head in agreement.

Daniel remounted to go look for the lost horse.

"Have you whistled for him? He may hear you and respond."

"No, I haven't, but what a good idea." He turned his horse around and let out a loud long whistle.

They stood stock still and listened. Seconds later they heard a whinny that seemed to come from the other side of the hill.

Daniel turned himself in his saddle and looked over at Anuta. He smiled gently, spurred his horse and waved goodbye as he rode off.

Anuta could scarcely believe that this eighteen-year-old young man for whom she had such deep feelings had come because of a wayward horse and professed his feelings for her. Because her own parents had suffered from an arranged marriage, she knew there were no behind-the-scenes arrangements being made. She decided it was time to talk to her parents about it.

She picked all the ripe berries from that bush, found another patch nearby, picked them clean and headed home. Her thoughts raced. *How will I break this to my parents? After all, I am the queen of being transparent with my feelings.* Over and over she rehearsed the conversation in her mind. She fervently hoped they would receive it well.

When she rode up to the house, Tanya was hanging laundry on the line. Anuta called for her, handed down the bucket of

114

berries and asked her to take it into the house. She needed to get the horse into the barn and unsaddle him.

Her parents were sitting at the kitchen table whispering to each other as Anuta walked into the house. They waved her over, and her father pointed to a chair. She braced herself for bad news.

"Oh, my little Anuta, you are now a young lady. In two more years you will be old enough to marry."

"Oh, no," she thought, "an arranged marriage."

"I am in love with Daniel," she blurted out. *Well, there goes my practiced speech!*

Her parents both started. Alixey smiled and silently shook his head.

Anuta thought the silence dragged on forever.

"Daniel left here a little while ago. It seems he feels the same about you. He would like to visit you in the evenings. And we approved. He says he intends to marry you. We told him he has to wait until you are sixteen."

"Oh, thank you, Mama and Papa!" Anuta responded joyfully.

"If he continues to visit, we'll know how serious he is. Please don't rush into anything, my darling," her mother advised her. "Don't try to grow up too fast."

Anuta hugged both her parents and thanked them for their advice and understanding.

That evening Daniel came over and visited Anuta while she sat at the sewing machine and made Katiya, her little sister, a dress.

For the next two years he came by to visit or to take Anuta and Tanya and Feta for a wagon ride. With each passing month they grew deeper in love. It seemed her sixteenth birthday would never arrive. But at last, one evening Daniel and his parents came over to properly propose and set a wedding date.

After all the arrangements and agreements were made, Daniel and his parents left. Tanya announced to her parents that there was a boy she really liked and that after Anuta's wedding was over, he was going to come over to talk to them about visiting.

To Anya it seemed as if just yesterday the three of them were waiting in the dugout for Alixey to return with the family. Now her two young ladies were preparing to fly the coop. She was grateful that both of these young suitors were raised well and had great values; her daughters would be cherished and loved and not used or abused as some women are. She had to open her arms and let them go even though Anuta was—and Tanya would be—required to live in the village. Family looks out for family. It was an unwritten rule.

Invariably the whole village got involved in every wedding. The men would put up a celebration hall. Some of the women would help with the cooking and baking, making chicken and venison noodle soup the day before the wedding while others helped to make clothes for the bride and groom. The bride's dress was colorful and bright, reflecting her happiness. Usually the groom dressed to match the bride's attire. Both of their outfits were embroidered with colorful threads.

The young bridesmaids, referred to as the friends, kept a constant watch over the bride in case someone else who was secretly in love with her would try to kidnap and have his way with her. She would then be obligated to marry him. In Anuta's memory it had happened twice. One girl was taken willingly because she did not like the young man her parents chose for her. The other girl objected, but he took her anyway. After he had had his way with her, the groom did not want her anymore. She had to marry her abductor and eventually learned to love him. He was good to her, and she finally settled into the marriage.

Anuta did not want to suffer any underhandedness, so she welcomed having her young lady friends surrounding her at all times. One slept beside her, and the others slept on the floor.

The evening before the wedding, Anuta and her friends went to the bath house along with her sister Tanya as an additional guardian. On their way home three young men jumped out from behind the bushes and grabbed Anuta, intending to carry her away. She started screaming and biting.

Tanya was a little bit taller than Anuta and still a tomboy. She, too, started hitting and kicking the young hooligans. When all the rest of the girls came to Anuta's rescue, the would-be abductors ran off. No one could clearly see their faces in the darkness, but Tanya knew they would be found out the next day. She fought hard and was confident that she had left bruises.

Alixey and Anya heard the screaming and so did her uncles from next door. They all came running, just in time to see the three young men sprint off. Daved and Petro gave chase but the boys were faster and got away.

Throughout the long night, the young friends took turns sitting awake guarding the bride lest there be another attempt on her.

Nor did Anuta's parents sleep soundly. They were too angry, regardless of whether this was a real abduction or a mere prank. They had seen the love that the couple had for one another and wanted their daughter to have happy peaceful memories of her wedding eve.

Morning came at last. Though still tired, the whole household was confident that the culprits would be found out at the church ceremony. They could not avoid going save due to death or severe illness; if they failed to show up at the church, they would be discovered by their absences. Either way, Alixey and Anya knew, they would be disciplined by the pastor and their own parents.

The friends dressed Anuta, who hardly touched her breakfast, decorated the wagon with bright ribbons and headed to the church. Upon their approach they heard people's voices calling to Daniel: "Your bride is approaching."

Anuta, now over her anxiety, rejoiced that in a little while she would be referred to as his wife.

Alixey's brothers had already arrived. They immediately came over and helped the bride and her friends down from the wagon. Four friends walked ahead of her and four behind. The party walked in to see Daniel waiting up front, radiating such love. It reminded Alixey and Anya of their own wedding.

The pastor had already decided how to handle the kidnapping attempt, of which word had spread through the whole village. He walked up front, looked at the attendants and noticed one man hanging his head. He cleared his throat and asked everyone to take a seat and quiet down. Anuta and her family took their seats in the back. Daniel sat down up front.

"It has come to my attention," Nikolai said loudly and clearly, "that three young men tried to disrupt the nuptials last evening." He pointed to the young man whose head was still bowed. "Philip, look up at me," Nikolai commanded him.

Philip hesitated for a moment, and then lifted up his head, exposing a black eye.

"How did you get your eye bruised?" Nikolai asked.

"I don't remember," Philip answered timidly.

"Could it have happened last night?"

Philip just shrugged his shoulders.

"Who were your accomplices?"

Philip remained silent, looking down at his feet.

Two young men stood up. Grigoriy had a split lip that was swollen, and Maxim appeared to be unharmed.

"Come up to the front," Nikolai told them.

Philip stood, and all three started up front. Maxim was limping. Tanya had been observing all this; she cupped her hand over her face and quietly laughed. She was proud of herself for fighting so hard for her sister.

Anuta looked over at her sister and smiled. She too was proud of her.

The three young men stood up front facing the crowd.

"Anyone want to question these men?" Nikolai asked.

Daniel stood. He was angry at them.

"Why?! Tell me why you committed such a crime?"

"We just wanted to pull a prank. We weren't going to hurt anyone. We just wanted to have a little fun," answered Maxim.

"Fun! Well, would you please ask Anuta, her family and her friends if they had any fun in all this? Look at how tired they all look; they do not look like they had any fun at all." Daniel stood there glaring at them.

Alixey was so proud of Daniel. He knew Anuta had made a very good choice.

Nikolai interrupted, "All right, you three, apologize to everyone, and if it will be all right with your parents I would like to sentence you."

The parents of the young men stood up. They were all in agreement with Nikolai. Alixey and Anya were their friends and they were ashamed of their sons' display of such foolishness.

"I think these men should clean up during and after the wedding." He looked up at Anya and Alixey and then at Suzanna and Mikhail, Daniel's parents. "Is that all right with all of you?" he asked.

"Yes," all four replied, nodding their heads.

"And how do the parents of these men feel?"

They all stood and agreed with the pastor's pronouncement.

"Teach these boys a lesson," called out the mother of one of the boys.

Anya felt remorse for the parents. What if Mark had done this? How would she feel? She wanted to say something, but this was not the time, so she kept quiet.

"Go ahead, boys, apologize," Nikolai ordered them.

They looked at one another and then at Anuta and her parents. Grigoriy and Philip leaned into Maxim who was standing between them and both whispered something to him.

Maxim cleared his throat and spoke up. "I am the one who came up with the idea. I talked Grigoriy and Philip into doing this. We originally were going to jump out of the bushes and yell Boo! just to startle them. But for some reason we decided to go one step further, and we grabbed Anuta. Tanya pounded on us, and we sport the bruise, split lip and limp. We deserve that and even more, so Anuta, Uncle Alixey and Aunt Anya, please accept our apologies. We will gladly bear our penalty and clean up during and after the ceremony. But please forgive us, and after we carry out our penance, please do not hold it against us, and do not blame our parents." Then he looked over at Tanya, smiled and said, "Hey, Tanya, thanks for the right cross, the elbow and the kick."

The whole congregation, including Anuta's and Daniel's parents, erupted into laughter.

Nikolai, still laughing, walked over to the three young men and told them to take their seats.

"Daniel and Anuta, please come up here," he requested.

Daniel stood and walked over to the pastor.

Anya, after Anuta had stood so her father could escort her to the front, took her by the shoulders, turned her toward herself and gave her a long hug. She quietly spoke these endearing words, "You are leaving me to start your own life, and I hope I have instilled enough in you to be able to stand on your own and be a good wife and mother." Both she and Anuta were tearful as she released her.

Anuta turned to her father, who wrapped his arms around her, held her and spoke a blessing over her. "You are my firstborn and you've brought your mother and me a lot of joy. You have always respected and obeyed us. May your children be the same. May your marriage be full of love and laughter and may your home always be a happy one." Then he kissed her on the cheek and gave her his arm. She placed her arm around his and they walked to the front.

"Who gives Anuta to Daniel on this day?" asked Nikolai.

"I do," answered her father. He leaned over to Anuta and gave her one more kiss on the cheek before turning to go back to his seat. As the vows were spoken Alixey and Anya shed many tears. They were so very happy for Anuta and Daniel but sad that she was no longer their little girl but a wife and daughter-in-law.

After the ceremony everyone was invited to the celebration hall where many tables groaned under the weight of all sorts of food. When everyone was seated, Suzanna and Mikhail and Daniel's side of the family hosted the reception. Always the groom's family performed that duty.

Wine was served during the meal, and since this was a May wedding and too early for berries, the wine was brewed from crushed wheat and honey. It went down good but had the kick of a mule.

Weddings usually lasted one week. The celebrations ended at dusk and resumed at breakfast. During the week the groom and his bride were given gifts. The drunker the guests got the more they gave. Some gave livestock, some gold. Others brought household items. Alixey and Anya gave the happy couple some of their land. Daved and Petro promised to help build their house and gave them a cow and chickens.

It was customary for a groom and his new wife to live with his parents until their house could be built. Anuta soon learned a few things about her mother-in-law. Not at all like her own mother, Suzanna was lazy and complained about everything. Anuta tried but could never please her. One day, after her mother-in-law almost hit her, she had had enough. She asked Daniel to start working on their new house.

He himself had heard enough of his mother's negative remarks. He loved her, but he knew she would never change. His father was hen-pecked and found things to do just to avoid her. Knowing what his wife had undergone, he solicited the help of Anuta's relatives and other men in the village to build a cozy two-bedroom single story home with the possibility of adding on later.

Anuta had her own home at last and made it a very cozy nest where she and her husband were very happy, lacking only children. They were inseparable and loved doing everything together. Daniel loved Anuta's family. He soon went to work for her father in the grain mill.

Stepan, the handsome quiet man Anuta thought hard to get to know but that Tanya loved, married her when she turned sixteen. He was very good to her, and they were very happy. He, too, went to work for his father-in-law, while Tanya enjoyed working in the home that had been built for them about two kilometers away. Their son Dima was born less than a year later.

It wasn't long before Anuta also became pregnant. Unlike Tanya's, hers was a long hard pregnancy. Alixey and Anya were concerned about her. She was very sensitive to smells and lost her appetite. By the time she gave birth to little Anya, she was skin and bones.

Alixey and Anya were now proud grandparents of two little ones, who seemed to grow so fast, and soon they were crawling and then walking.

Everyone in Chubaroyka was thriving; the livestock were multiplying, and life was wonderful with weddings and new children coming into the world. Each new home built meant more cleared fertile land; the villagers grew plenty of healthy crops for themselves and to sell. All seemed tranquil. No one knew the silent enemy that was about to strike this picturesque village with tears and mourning.

15

Death

One night Alixey and Anya had put their children to bed and were doing their quiet evening chores. Anya was at the sewing machine making a dress for Lara, and Alixey was making a pair of shoes out of deer hide for little Katiya. There was a loud knock at the door. Alixey did not call out for them to enter; he did not want to wake the children. He tiptoed over to the door and opened it. Masha and Vasili were standing there quietly, and Alixey stepped aside to let them in. "Come in! Have a seat at the dining room table. I will get Anya."

Vasili walked in first with Masha following. Both were quiet, their faces pale. Neither said a word, something very unusual for them. Always happy, with their presence they lit up any room that they entered.

Alixey was getting nervous. He went to let Anya know they had company. "Anya, Vasili and Masha are here. They are in the dining room," he told her just above a whisper.

"Oh, Masha and Vasili are here?" She left her sewing machine and headed into the kitchen to get refreshments for them. Alixey went to visit with his friends. He knew they had news and, by their expressions, he did not want to hear it.

124

"Masha, Vasili, what is going on? You are both so silent."
He sat down with them.

"We bring news." Vasili was somber.

Anya walked into the room bringing a tray of refreshments.
She was silent and knew this was something serious. Her knees
felt weak. Her hands were shaking as she set tea cups in front of
everyone. She almost dropped the teapot when she started to
pour Masha's cup.

"Well," Vasili said, "I will wait for Anya to sit with us, then I
will deliver it to you."

Anya quickly pulled out a chair, set down the pot and sat.

"We just came back from visiting Masha's sister in Kum.
Smallpox is ravaging the village. They are carrying out two or
three dead people from each home. They have full time grave-
diggers. The cemetery is growing daily. I am afraid the same
thing will happen here. Masha's sister lost two children, and her
husband is sick."

Smallpox was no stranger to Alixey and Anya. It had gone
through their village when they were children. When this
invisible enemy attacked, it spared their homes but took over half
the population. When a human enemy came close, you could
duck and hide from him, but this... You never knew where it was
and whom it would strike next. It did not care whether you were
young or old, or whether your family needed you. It just
devoured like a ravenous beast.

Anya was too stunned to say a word. Would she lose any of
her family members? Or would her family lose her? Either way
there would grief and pain. Their little cemetery would claim all
whom this enemy would kill.

Everyone sat quietly. Nothing was spoken, and no one was
sipping his or her tea or touching the pastries.

Masha broke the silence with a question. "What do we do now?"

No one seemed to respond right away. It seemed that to speak would be to make one responsible for everyone.

Alixey finally cleared his throat. He felt as if something had a grip around it. "Well, I think we should send word to all our neighbors, and tomorrow night we should assemble at the church and pray. Perhaps somewhere we sinned against God and broke one of His laws, and He is sending punishment upon us."

Everyone agreed with Alixey and decided Vasili and Masha would go to the south end of the village while Alixey and his wife informed the north end. At that, Vasili and Masha stood up, gave their hosts a hug and wished a blessing on them. Their hosts in return blessed them, and they left without a word.

The next morning Anuta, Daniel and little Anya came over. They had been invited for breakfast the day before. The air in the house seemed laden with heaviness. Anuta sensed it and asked Anya, "Mama, what's wrong? I feel a heaviness in here."

Her mother looked up at her and answered, "We are all fine, but the news we received last evening was hard to hear."

"What news?"

"Smallpox."

"Smallpox? Who has smallpox?" Anuta was startled by this news. She had heard about the horrible illness and was worried. She turned around and looked at her husband. He was shocked as well. Neither one had experienced it or seen its aftermath.

Anuta did not want herself or any of her family members to die or be disfigured. Her voice now tension-filled and fearful, she asked, "Mama, who has smallpox?"

"No one in our village, but people are dying in Kum."

"But Kum is not that far away, Mama!" she answered.

Lara had been milking the cows, and Alixey was doing his morning chores. They both walked into the house at the same time. Lara set the bucket of milk on the counter and joined her older sister. She had heard part of the conversation but was still not sure what they were talking about.

Alixey walked into the room and broke up the conversation. "All right, everyone, let's have breakfast. We will talk more tonight when we assemble at church."

They all stood and faced the icons that were in the northeast corner of the dining room and prayed, crossed themselves and then bowed to them. When they were finished, everyone sat down around the long rectangular table and ate in somber silence.

Alixey knew their lives were never going to be the same again. Those who lived through this illness would bear the scars to prove it, and those who lost loved ones would have scars on their hearts.

The news was delivered throughout the whole village, and that night everyone gathered at the church to pray. They tried to live by God's law the best they could and hoped that he would withhold this punishment from them.

Two weeks later, Vasili became ill and developed flu-like symptoms. He became feverish and severely fatigued and complained of a terrible headache. Everyone hoped it was just influenza, but when the pus-filled blisters appeared all over his body, they knew it was what they all feared—smallpox.

With agonizing slowness it ravaged the whole village. Some recovered, others died. The cemetery had indeed claimed many lives.

Stepan, Tanya's husband, started to complain of symptoms. He was severely covered by the pus-filled blisters and died two weeks later.

Tanya was devastated. She cried so deeply that she ran out of tears. Anuta and Daniel had to help her to walk to the cemetery to bury him. When his grave had been filled with the soil, she fell on it and begged him to come back. She promised him that she would dig him back up with her bare hands if he would only get back up. When Tanya started digging up the dirt with her hands and pleading loudly for her husband to get up or take her with him, everyone at the grave site cried aloud.

Alixey and Anya were broken by the pain of their precious daughter, who at a very young age used to put her shoes on the wrong feet but was now saying goodbye to the one she loved. They wished they could take the pain from her. But there was nothing that they could do, so they just stood and cried with her.

Tanya had just decided she was through with living when suddenly she heard Dima cry; this pulled her back to reality. He needed her and was proof of the love that she and Stepan had shared. She stopped digging and just lay on top of the grave and sobbed. Her father gently came over to her and lifted her to her feet. They embraced each other and quietly sobbed together.

Three weeks later little Anya fell victim to the illness, and a week after that she died.

Anuta and Daniel held a tearful funeral for their little girl. They would miss this happy blue-eyed blonde. They did not know how to go on with their lives. Little Anya was such a huge part of it. Now there was just this emptiness. They were going to miss the little girl who used to crawl into bed with them in the middle of the night. Daniel loved to feel her breath on his neck when she fell asleep with her head on his shoulder. Whenever they went to visit friends and she got tired, she wanted him to hold her. How was he ever going to get over that?

Each time Alixey and Anya would see the toys with which she had played when she came over, there would be tears. Alixey found himself weeping several times a day over her. Natasha finally picked up the toys and put them where no one would stumble across them, feeling as if she were burying little Anya a second time.

Vasili recovered from the smallpox but had been scarred all over his body, his face not so badly as elsewhere. No one fell ill in Alixey's home; Petro, Daved and their mother were fine. Feodor and Fedosia both died. Simon, Nadiya and Leonid were all right. The epidemic finally vanished as mysteriously as it had appeared. As Alixey had predicted, everyone had fallen victim to this terrible beast and was scarred on their bodies, on their hearts or both. Most of the village suffered, and to recover from the losses took time, but eventually life got back to normal. People did the best they could without the ones they lost.

As every room reminded her of Stepan's absence, Tanya struggled, living by herself, though she frequently received help from family and friends.

Alixey and Anya saw how much she suffered. They talked her into moving back in with them and sold off her livestock but kept the wheat fields. They locked up the house and let it sit empty. Perhaps one of the other children would live in it someday. Or maybe Tanya would want to live there again.

Feta turned fifteen. A young man named Kiril took an interest in her and approached her parents. When they asked her about him, she did not want to get married, especially not to him; instead, she wanted to learn about herbs and their healing properties. She begged her parents to let her go and study with a Chinese doctor who had a little cabin in Kum where he treated people, but they were concerned for her safety. A lady would have to travel there and back every day, and she needed to be wary of bears and snakes and other creatures.

After a few weeks she met a family that had but one daughter her age. They invited her to come and stay with them, so Alixey and Anya went to meet them and gave their permission. Maxim and Feadora were excited to have met them, and their daughter Vassa was glad to have a friend.

Anuta had a little boy, Yoseph, and two years later another little girl they named Anya. (Anuta loved that name.) Yoseph was a mirror image of his father and loved to bang on things, just like his father did when he built or repaired things. He had to be closely watched; he was a fearless young man. Anya, on the other hand, was a quiet young lady. She was blonde and blue-eyed just like the sister she never met. Anuta adored her little family and spent much of the day doing things for them.

16
Murder

It had been a wonderful summer. The gardens were thriving; the root cellars were awaiting the harvest. The wheat was full of kernels and was almost ready to harvest.

Anuta tossed and turned in her sleep, soaking the sheets with sweat. A dense black fog hovered over the whole village, blanketing the ground. She looked around but could not see anyone through the thick clouds. She desperately ran here and there but her husband was nowhere to be found. She called and called, but he did not answer. Her son and daughter were by her side, but somehow her son disappeared. She sought him frantically but in vain. Anguished cries came from different areas of the village, but she could not tell from whom.

The dread in the pit of her stomach began to abate as she woke. She got out of bed and walked to the window. No, no fog. A beautiful sunrise painted cheerful colors on the sky as the sun peeked out from behind the trees. The azure sky was filled with birds greeting the day with joyous songs telling her to get up and get going to the river for water. The water splashing in the river seemed to say, *Come, bring your buckets!*

She dressed and headed out the door. The heavy fog, now invisible, hung only on her heart. Still the birds sang, the grass swayed in the breeze, and the river rippled. Yet the heaviness remained.

Daniel noticed that she seemed too quiet, so he questioned her.

"I have a feeling something bad is going to happen today," she told him.

"What do you think is going to happen?"

"I'm not sure, but I can't shake it loose. Mama and Papa and all the children are going to visit Feta at Maxim and Feadora's. They'll be gone a week. I hope they have a safe time. Maybe I'm just sad they're leaving," she replied.

Daniel walked over and gave her a comforting hug. He assured her the week would be over before she knew it. "I'm sure that's all it is, just the thought of them leaving," he told her.

Anuta put a pot of soup on the stove to simmer. She took Yoseph and Anya and went next door to her parents to say goodbye. They were packed and ready to go. Tanya would stay home to take care of the livestock and to do the daily chores.

Anuta gave everyone a hug and kiss and waved goodbye as they rode off in their creaking wagon, the same one that brought them over from Russia. As they drove out of sight and Tanya went back inside to fetch her son and a milk pail, she went to get her own pail. Yoseph and Anuta were quietly playing in the barn while she milked the cow when suddenly a strong surge of fear shot through her. She stood up, disturbed, though she hadn't finished the milking. She set the pail off to one side, told the children to stay in the barn and went out. What was going on here? Why was she feeling this? What was happening to her?

"Daniel, where are you?" she called out to him.

"I'm down by the river checking the fish basket," he called back. He, too, knew something was going on. He had a strange feeling that they needed to hide. But from whom were they supposed to hide? There was nothing to fear in this quiet village. He pulled the basket out of the water. In it were several fish for their dinner. He set it down on the riverbank and jogged toward the barn.

As always, when Anuta finished the milking, she set the pail on a small table out of the way, opened the stall and let the cows out into the corral. She picked up the pail and poured milk into the cat bowl to feed Murka's descendants. After all, those cats were needed to keep the mice population down.

Daniel came up and took the milk pail from her, and they started for the house. In the yard they found the reindeer that had been sold to Meernu some time back.

"Bobka and Domka, what are you doing here?" Anuta called out to them. "Daniel, they must have gotten loose. Take them back to Meernu."

Daniel saddled his horse, mounted, whistled to Bobka and Domka and called them. They hesitated, then started after him and followed as he rode ahead. He was terrified at what he saw when he arrived at Meernu's. All the family members lay on the ground side by side covered in blood. Their throats had been cut, and the women appeared to have been raped. The barn door was open and the animals gone. His horse could smell the blood and kept turning restlessly. Daniel could see by the hoof- and footprints that there had been several men. He turned around and galloped home without dismounting.

"Who did this gruesome crime? Why?" he asked himself, "And where are these people now? Who are they, and what was their motive?" When he finally got home he didn't even notice that the reindeer were right behind him. He dismounted before his horse came to a stop, ran to the house and ordered Anuta to lock the door. He told her he would be right back.

Anuta had never before heard him use that tone of voice. She ran out the door and saw the reindeer in the yard again. "Daniel, what is happening?" she called after him as he ran toward his parents' house.

He spun around and replied abruptly. "Anuta, get inside and lock the door, now!" He turned again, sprinted to his in-laws' and burst in through the door. "Tanya!" he shouted, "Tanya, where are you?"

"I am upstairs," her voice called back.

"Tanya, get your son and come down, quickly," he ordered her. She hurried to the top of the stairs and could see that he meant what he said.

"What is it?"

"Come down now. There is danger about. You must come to our house, now!"

Tanya called, "Dima, my son, we are going to Yoseph and Anya's house. Come on, let's go."

Daniel could hear the pitter-patter of little feet as Dima appeared at the top of the stairs by his mother's side. Tanya took his hand, and together they descended the stair. When they got to the bottom step, Daniel took Tanya by the arm, led them outside and closed the door behind them.

Tanya was deeply concerned. "What is going on, Daniel?" she asked, her voice cracking.

"Let's get inside, then we'll talk."

As they approached the door, Anuta, who had been watching through the window, pulled the door open and let them in.

After everyone was inside, Daniel closed and locked the door behind them. He asked the children to go play quietly in the family room and took the women to the dining room. When they were seated, he looked at Anuta then at Tanya without saying a word. These were young ladies; they were not supposed to be worrying about things such as killings. They had barely healed from losing their family members to smallpox. How would they take this news, especially with their parents away?

"What is going on, Daniel?" Anuta demanded.

"Meernu and his family have been murdered," Daniel blurted out, surprising himself at the delivery. Both women were shocked. This was a small peaceful village. Nothing bad was supposed to happen, not here, not in this village.

The ladies just sat, stunned.

"How could this be?" Anuta asked.

"This is unbelievable," Tanya added.

All three sitting around the table trying to make sense of it all hoped that this was an isolated incident and that it would not happen to anyone else.

Anuta smelled the aroma of the soup and got up to add the potatoes and carrots. Suddenly there was a loud knock at the door. Everyone jumped in terror. Four-year-old Yoseph ran to his father. Six-year-old Dima led his two-year-old cousin Anya by the hand.

Anuta tiptoed to the window to see who it was that knocked so violently. She pulled back the curtain ever so slightly and gasped. "Daniel, there are several armed men out there," she said just above a whisper, hoping they did not hear her.

Daniel stood up to get the door. Anuta did not remember ever being so frightened. She begged him not to.

He did not want to answer but feared the consequences would be much worse if he didn't. Suddenly someone delivered a hard kick to the door, and it flew open. The children ran screaming to their parents. Anuta grabbed them as the men rushed into their home. She did the best she could to comfort them; she was terrified herself.

Dima stood silently at his mother's side as she tried to still her racing heart. Tanya could not believe this was really happening. Fearing the men would become more agitated, she went over to Anuta to help her with the little ones.

"Why are you here? What do you want?" Daniel asked the man who seemed to be in charge.

"We want all of you outside," the man ordered.

Still confused and dazed, they all headed for the door, the children crying.

"Shut them up right now or will shut them up for you," the same man roared as his cold black eyes flared.

Anuta picked up Anya, Daniel picked up Yoseph, and they went outside. As they went out Anuta remembered her soup and turned to go back to the kitchen. A man grabbed her by the sash around her waist and almost yanked her off her feet.

"My soup, I need to take it off the stove," she yelled.

"Leave it and get out," he screamed.

Daniel, remembering what had seen in Meernu's front yard, was terrified. He could not bear the thought of something like that happening to his family. He quietly prayed, asking God to at least spare the women and children. It was clear to him that this was a gang of murderous thugs, probably the Tartars. They were not just one nationality. There were Russians, Mongols and Turks, all speaking Russian.

"What do you want from us?" he asked.

"We are cleaning scum off the earth for Muhammad."

"We are not scum, we are simple farmers. We are not bothering anyone; we keep to ourselves. Please leave us alone," Anuta said loudly, hearing the terror in her own voice.

"Shut up!" the same man roared again. "Speak again and you will be shot."

Anuta, remembering her dream, knew she was going to lose her husband and perhaps her own life to these terrible men. She began sobbing as she went over to her husband, put her arm around his and put her head on his chest.

Daniel tried to comfort her, but he knew what the outcome would be.

The men ordered them to walk to the village square. As they did, they prayed to God to give them courage for what they were about to undergo.

As they walked out of the yard and onto the dirt road, they saw their neighbors being led at gunpoint in the same direction. Daniel saw his parents, and Anuta saw her uncles Simon, Daved and Petro along with their wives and children. Some women were silent; others were wailing. The children were all frightened. Some lay on the ground screaming, some had their hands wrapped around their parents' legs or waists. It tore Anuta's heart in all directions as it pounded so hard she thought it would burst.

Tanya was the strong one both emotionally and physically. She saw how distracted her sister was. She walked up to her and wrapped her arm around Anuta's waist as all three walked, with Dima hanging onto his mother's dress.

"Maybe they are just trying to intimidate us. Maybe they will just leave," Tanya whispered into Anuta's ear.

"I hope so," Anuta whispered back.

When they reached the square, orders were issued for the men to stand side by side single file facing their families. The women were to stand off to the side and watch, and the Tartars were to get in their formation and to take aim. Knowing what was about to happen, all the women began screaming and begging them to stop.

The marauders took aim and stood silently waiting for the order.

Daniel was still, gazing out at his wonderful wife and lovely children as tears ran down his face.

"Fire!" someone shouted. Shots rang out. Daniel and most of the men went down. The Tartars reloaded their weapons; again the rifles cracked, and the rest of the men went down. Smoke and the smell of gunpowder hung in the air. A third time the Tartars reloaded as the women and children screamed. Some tried to run to their men but were violently shoved back.

The Tartars walked over to the men and fired point-blank into them to make sure that they were dead. Some women, their children clinging to them, stood and cried. Others fell to their knees; their legs gave out on them from the terrible sight. Anuta fainted and dropped to the ground as her two screaming children clung to her.

Suddenly Anuta felt a sharp pain in her jaw and opened her eyes to see a Mongolian-looking man bent over her.

"Get up!" he ordered.

She struggled to get up as Tanya quickly stepped over and pulled her to her feet. Anuta fell into her sister's arms and wept. Struck dumb by all the grief, she could only cry.

Tanya took her by the shoulders, pulled away from her and in a commanding voice ordered her to get it together. "Look at your son; he is so grief-stricken that he can't even cry. We need to help him, or he will go into shock."

Anuta, attempting to comfort Yoseph, set her own grief aside and swept him into her arms. He was not responding but was limp and pale.

Dima had curled up into a ball on the ground and wept after witnessing his grandfather and uncles murdered. Now he stood up and went to help with Yoseph.

Pulled from the Ashes: Murder

Tanya was like a rock. She made up her mind to fall apart later. Right now she needed to help her sister and the children to stay alive. She was also concerned about Vassa, who with her husband had moved to the village about a month earlier. Vassa's baby was due any day now, and she could go into labor from all this trauma.

The Tartars talked amongst themselves for a few moments, and then ordered the women to start marching north.

An older woman spoke up. "Where are you taking us? We have young children and a pregnant woman here."

One man walked up to her and glared into her face. He pulled a knife out of its sheath, stabbed her in the heart, and she fell to the ground, dead.

"What are you doing?" shouted his commander.

"My knife was thirsty for blood, but now it's fine," came his reply.

"Get these women and their children in a group and ready to go," came the command.

Some of the women had to be lifted to their feet by their friends and relatives. Everyone was silent. They saw what was done to those who asked questions. Not knowing what their fate would be, their only hope was God. They knew the murders were the fault of these evil men and not His. Silently they prayed.

A man appeared with all the horses belonging to the Tartars. The men mounted and again ordered the women to follow. The women quietly and fearfully obeyed as half of the men rode ahead, half behind.

Little Anya, who was being carried by her aunt, complained of hunger. Tanya picked berries along the way and handed them to her.

Yoseph also had to be carried. Anuta quietly whispered to him, trying to get him to talk, but he just moaned. His grief was so great that his life was slowly draining out of him. Anuta had to fight the tears, and when she was losing, desperate for him to be all right and afraid to talk to him, she would turn her head so her son could not see them.

Tanya handed little Anya to a woman walking beside her and took Yoseph and carried him. He was burning up with a fever. She knew if he did not come out of it, he would be dead soon, so she hummed to him as they walked.

Tired, thirsty and hungry, the women and children kept up the pace. It was clear to them that these bloodthirsty men needed very little provocation, so they complied with all of their rules; they continued to put one foot in front of the other, grimly trudging toward who knew what. When one man suddenly bellowed, "Kill anyone who stumbles!" the situation became clear; they were no more than game to be hunted, worn down so as to kill off the weak ones first. So they locked elbows and held each other up as they walked. As the daylight faded away at last, and the night got too dark to see, they were ordered to sit on the ground in a group. The fear was now so thick that it had swallowed them.

Along the way, Yoseph died. Tanya, afraid her sister would fall apart and collapse and become a victim herself, did not say a word to her.

When everyone was finally seated, Anuta asked Tanya about Yoseph. "Oh, he finally fell asleep," she told her.

"Let me take him," Anuta requested.

"No, no, leave him be. He is just fine in my arms. Take care of Anya," Tanya replied.

The men gathered wood and built a fire. Some of them went out to the woods, shot some game, cooked it over the fire and ate it. No one offered any to the women and children.

"You might as well get some sleep; we head out at daylight," the commander barked at them.

Anuta took Anya from the woman that had been carrying her and thanked her. She found a spot on the ground, lay down and waited till her daughter was asleep. Then she quietly cried herself to sleep.

Tanya laid Yoseph's body on the ground and lay down beside him. She finally let herself get emotional like her sister and cried herself to sleep as well. She dreamt that she and Anuta were cleaning house. No matter how much they mopped the floor, they could not get it clean. Suddenly a crow let out a loud squawk and woke her up. She opened her eyes and saw the still body of her nephew beside her. She looked over at her sister who was just starting to wake up. Sitting up, she saw a smoldering campfire. The men were gone. She didn't know whether they had left or were hiding behind trees ready to shoot them like sitting ducks, but she knew she had to tell her sister that her son was dead and dreaded every moment.

Anuta sat up and asked about Yoseph.

Tanya broke into tears and confessed, "Anuta, my dear sister, he died in my arms while we were walking yesterday. I just could not bring myself to tell you."

Anuta started wailing. She did not care if anyone heard her. "They killed my Daniel and my Yoseph. They are not human. If it were not a sin to curse them, I would," she screamed over her sobbing.

Anuta's mother-in-law got up on all fours, crawled over and slowly reached out and touched Yoseph's cold body. She bent down close to him and started to lament over her grandson. Anuta and Tanya joined her while Dima sat off to the side and quietly wept. He was going to miss his spirited cousin. They were very close and played together all the time. Now he was with his father.

Vassa was sitting quietly and weeping. Suddenly she started moaning and got up on her knees. She looked down on the ground. Her dress and the area where she had been sitting were wet. "What's happening with me?" she called out.

Several women rushed to the side of the laboring woman.

Anuta cried until there were no more tears. She had to bury her son in these woods. A short distance away she picked up a stick and started digging. Her sister and Dima soon joined her and they dug a shallow grave. Anuta took her undergarment and used it to wrap her son's body. Afterward, they lowered it into the grave and all again broke into weeping.

Anuta could go on no longer; she had no strength left. "Goodbye, my son. Go be with your father. We will meet again someday," she said to his lifeless body, and she started pushing the earth over her little boy. That done, rocks were piled on top, followed by branches so no animal would be able to dig him up.

17

Rescue

Vassa was now in labor. She had had nothing to eat the day before and needed strength to get through the birth. Some of the women went to dig edible roots and others to pick berries to feed the new mother. Certain the cruel men would appear at any moment, they nevertheless had more pressing business. The contractions became rapidly closer and closer, and soon she started to push. The midwife shouted, "Vassa, you have a son!" Vassa covered her face with both hands as the tears rolled down her face. Her husband did not get to meet the son he wanted, and the son would have to grow up without his father. The midwife asked for a kindhearted woman to donate her undergarments in which to wrap the baby.

That done, the women had to find water and something to eat. They were not sure where they were, but they retraced their steps, following the plentiful tracks that they had left getting there. Two at a time they took turns helping Vassa walk. The threat of the tigers and bears deep in these woods kept them moving; the noise and the scent of the newborn might attract something. Everyone hoped they would happen upon a stream. They were silently walking along when they heard the clang,

clang of horses. They all ran for cover while one woman peeked out to see who was coming. "Soldiers!" she cried out.

When they stood and yelled for help, the soldiers quickly rode over to them.

"What are you women doing here?" the commander called.

"We are from Chubaroyka. The Tartars have executed our men and driven us into these woods," Anuta's mother-in-law answered. "We have a young woman here who gave birth a little while ago. We need a horse for her," she continued.

The commander ordered some of the men to escort the women back to their homes. With them was an extra horse that they had found grazing out in the meadow.

Anuta recognized it. "That is my horse. He must have run off during the gunfire," she called out.

"Six men will escort you back to your village. We will give you some of our food, and you will be taken to a stream. We are hunting those same Tartars. They have invaded several villages and have killed many people."

The women were grateful to God for sending the soldiers. Now they had a chance of getting home safely. The task of burying their husbands was waiting for them. They had never dug graves and dreaded the thought of putting their family members into them. Their hearts were numb, and their faces were burning from the salty tears.

Six soldiers, knowing it might be just them against the Tartars, volunteered for the duty. But they themselves had wives, sisters and mothers and shuddered at the thought of them having to face what these women had been through. They checked their ammunition supply, took food for the ladies, helped Vassa up on Anuta's horse, handed her the baby and started off.

Anuta was leaving her son in the woods. She called his name over and over again as she walked. Her face was once again soaked with tears; she had cried so much that she could barely see. Tanya walked up and took her by the arm and helped her keep her footing.

It was a long walk home. The soldiers left to go back to their platoon as soon as the women reached the village.

The cows were in their corral mooing in pain from overfilled udders. Anya's front door hung crooked from being kicked in, but those were not high priorities. Their men's bodies still lay where they fell; they had to be buried. Anuta and Tanya asked Dima to watch Anya while they carried out the burdensome task.

The women determined that Daniel and his father would be laid to rest side by side. Simon, Daved, and Petro would be by Feodor and Fedosia. Not a single man remained in the village. Vasili, Masha and their children were visiting relatives. Oseph, Zenya and their daughter Zina were away and were spared, as was Simon's son Leonid. The seventeen-year-old had been mistaken for a child and ordered to stand with the women. He would be available to help them dig graves.

Lanterns were lit to help them see in the gathering dark. One by one the graves were dug. No one was able to build coffins; instead, the bodies were wrapped in blankets, lowered into the shallow graves and covered with earth. The toilsome work dragged on almost until morning. It was just as well. No one could have slept.

Tanya, tired and afraid the Tartars would return, still had to take care of Anuta, who after she completed their routine chores fell into an illness brought on by all the grief. She held hands with her and the children. Tanya could not leave her sister by herself to go get her parents so she suffered in silence, doing her best to act cheerful for everyone's sake.

News of the terrible ordeal reached Kum. Alixey heard of it and quickly set out for home, driving the horses as fast they could safely go. As he and his family approached the village and saw all the new graves in the cemetery, the news slowly sank in. It was all too real; the men had been killed. Anya began sobbing for all who had lost loved ones.

Tanya was walking out of the barn carrying a pail of milk when her family pulled up to the house. She dropped the pail. Milk splashed all over. She fell to her knees and began to sob like a little child.

Anya was the first one off the wagon. She ran to her daughter, fell to her knees, grabbed her, and they held each other as they both wailed.

Tanya started hyperventilating from the sobbing. Her father got down on his knees at her side and tried to comfort her. Finally she drew a full breath and was able to speak. "They killed Daniel, Uncles Simon, Daved, and Petro. We buried them two days ago without coffins. Yoseph died from the grief. We buried him in a shallow grave in a wooded area a day's walk from here. Anuta is sick from grief. I am afraid she may die."

Alixey, filled with hatred and grief at the same time, stood up and walked away. He needed time to get himself together. Their peaceful village had been tainted with death and sorrow far worse than the smallpox epidemic. He had to go see his Anuta and help her.

Anuta was in bed. Pale and with sunken-in eyes, she looked as if she were not breathing, but she opened and closed her eyes as her father walked in. Realizing who was standing over her, she opened them again and lethargically sat up. She reached out and took his hand. Pressing it against her face, she began weeping.

He wept with her. Not even twenty-five, she already had suffered the loss of so many loved ones.

After catching her breath, she cried out through her sobbing, "They killed my Daniel and Yoseph. How can I go on? Can anyone tell me?"

Alixey wiped his own tears away and found his voice. "You have a lovely little girl who needs her mother."

"Yes, I do." Anuta slowly nodded. "Yes, she does need me." She got out of bed, gave her father a long hug, and asked about the rest of the family.

"They are all outside," Alixey answered. "Get dressed and come out into the sunshine. I know how much pain you are in. We are all hurting, but for our little ones we have to keep going. Get dressed. I'll wait for you at the top of the stairs and walk you out." He went out of the room and closed the door behind him.

Anuta walked over to the window and looked out, her heart weighed down with sorrow. The sky was blue. The trees gently swayed in the breeze and the birds chirped. Normally this would have lifted her spirit but not today, not for a long time.

Alixey and Tanya hitched the horses to the wagon, loaded a little coffin on the back and set out to bring back little Yoseph to give him a proper burial. The whole village came together to hold a memorial service for him and for all who had perished.

The villagers later heard that all the gang members had been hunted down and executed by firing squad, but people continued to be fearful as they heard rumors of other groups forming and massacring.

18
Defense

Almost two years had passed since the massacre. Tanya met Sergey, a young man who, though scarred from head to toe from the smallpox, was nonetheless a very kind and gentle man who loved Tanya and Dima. He asked Tanya to marry him. After the wedding she sold her home and property, and he moved her to his village. The house was not large like the one in Chubaroyka, but she was happy there with its broad wheat fields and twenty-two beehives that produced abundant honey. The surrounding mountains were peaceful, with wild onions, rhubarb and wild fruits and berries growing all around.

Arsalon was a small village named after the Arsalon River, a tributary of the Kosh. The Kosh was a wide white-water river; the current was quick and dangerous. Only the skilled attempted to cross it. The natural barriers of the Kosh on one side and the mountains on the other three sides of the village served to protect it from certain groups.

Reports of villages being attacked made people back in Chubaroyka nervous. They felt like sitting ducks with no natural protection from any direction. One morning a woman rode into town. She was not making sense, but by her speech they knew she was from a small village nestled on a plateau with a cliff on one side. She said something about being attacked and everyone being thrown from the cliff rather than being shot. Pregnant women were cut open, and the fetuses were impaled on spears, then thrown from the cliff with their mothers. She had hidden under a large washtub, occasionally looking out to see the brutal murders. Certain they would come back through the village and find her, she spent the rest of that day and night cramped under the tub, too terrified to come out. The screams and cries drove her near to insanity. When she was confident that they had gone, she climbed out, found a horse they must have missed and left. She rode all day and happened upon Chubaroyka.

Her story sent waves of shock through all the people. A few, who knew how to get there, volunteered to check the story out. They armed themselves, took enough supplies and headed off. Several days later they returned with stories more gruesome than what they had been told. They had buried everyone in shallow graves and returned home. On their way back they stopped at a store and bought bells.

A town assembly was called and it was decided that every household would have a bell erected on a pole. With any sign of danger, it would be rung, and any able-bodied men and women would arm themselves to defend their village.

One morning while Anuta was milking her cow, her father walked into the barn. He looked very concerned. She saw this and asked, "What is it, Papa? Why do you look so concerned?"

He took a deep breath and let out a sigh. "Oh, my Anuta, I was getting water for the cows and met up with Fadey. He informed me that his granddaughter has cholera."

Anuta was hoping that she had heard him wrong. "Now, could you please repeat that, Papa?" she asked as she continued to milk her cow.

Alixey knew how fragile she had become after the grief she
had experienced. He hesitated a moment and repeated himself.
"Fadey's granddaughter has cholera."

Anuta, now done with the milking, stood up, placed the pail
on the table and opened the stall to let the cow out into the corral.
Then she turned back to her father and spoke clearly. "Well,
Papa, God will give us the strength to get through it. I tried to
give up once, only to find that we have to go on no matter what
happens."

Alixey smiled, walked over to her, gave her a hug and kissed
her cheek. "We have each other, and with God's help we will get
through it. You are right." He hoped she would never again
suffer the loss of loved ones. She was one that loved deeply and
hurt deeply. He took the bucket of milk, poured some into the
cats' bowl and carried the rest into her kitchen. She still needed to
collect the eggs and feed the chickens. After telling her, "Oh,
Anuta, I will send Natasha and Lara to help you water the cows,"
he left.

A few days later little Anya became ill. Diarrhea flowed out
of her like yellow water. She must have known she was going to
die. She kept telling her mother how much she loved her. Very
hot to the touch, she kept asking for water, but the more she
drank, the more it ran out of her. One week later she died in her
sleep with her whole family gathered around her.

Anuta did not cry. Instead she felt her heart harden. She
prepared her little Anya's body for burial. Her father built a little
coffin. They buried her in the cemetery not far from her father,
and Anuta had not shed a tear. Her father assured her worried
mother that in time the tears and healing would come. A week
went by: no tears.

Then one morning Anuta rushed into her parents' house.
Her father came over to greet her. She fell into his arms and

sobbed inconsolably while he continued to hold her. After the tears would no longer flow, she just whimpered. Her heart was broken beyond human repair, and her parents knew this. She would never be the sweet loving Anuta they knew. She had become withdrawn and depressed. She had lost her whole family. They knew she could not live by herself anymore, so they moved her in with them and sold her home.

Misha, one of the soldiers who had volunteered to escort the women back to the village when they were taken to the woods by the Tartars, had noticed how beautiful Anuta was. He asked one of the women about her and was told that she had just lost her husband. He decided he would check on her in two years after he had served his time and was discharged.

The Tartar uprising had been suppressed; those who remained returned to their homeland. Muslim fundamentalists, even more numerous and ruthless than the Tartars, were now terrorizing the countryside.

Misha's father was a general in Tsar Nicholas's army and was a decorated hero for saving the Tsar's life. One day the Tsar sat with his military advisers in a conference room working out a plan of defense against the Bolsheviks. Someone broke the glass out of a window and threw in an armed grenade. Some of the men dove under the table while others ran out of the room. Kiril ran up to the grenade and threw it back out of the window. He threw himself on the Tsar as a human shield. The grenade exploded on the other side of the wall; pieces of it flew into the room and pelted Kiril, but the Tsar was spared. Everyone applauded him for his bravery, and that same day Tsar Nicholas promoted him to a general and awarded him a large gold cross encrusted with gems.

Later, after the Tsar was overthrown, there was a bounty put out on all his officers, including Kiril. One autumn night he hid in a ditch half filled with water and almost froze to death. Becoming very ill, he made it home only to be diagnosed with pneumonia. A few days later he died, leaving his wife Anna and five children behind.

They were shunned by most people because of Kiril's loyalty to the Tsar. Taking only the bare necessities, they snuck into China. Misha was only twelve years of age. After they settled in to a home that Misha helped to build, his mother lost the use of her legs. It was said she had become overwhelmed with grief and given up on life. A year later she died.

Misha, now fourteen, was the sole support for his siblings. He had to become an adult at a very young age. His sister Anna was twelve, Irina was ten, Ganya nine and his brother Maxim seven. They never went without food. Misha had learned to hunt and fish when he was ten years old. His uncle Ivan used to take him out into the woods and streams.

Misha was twenty-one when he was drafted into the military. His commander took an interest in him and his sharpshooting abilities. Within a short time he was sent on ambushes. Misha carried out all his orders: it was shoot or be shot.

He hated what he had become. In his own eyes he was a legal murderer; those he killed lay heavy on his heart. One late afternoon his regiment fought a pitched battle with a battalion of Muslims, eventually killing all but one who had been hiding under a few dead comrades. When he thought it safe, he ran but was spotted, overtaken and mounted on a horse with his hands tied behind his back. Misha was ordered to take him over the next hill and execute him. As he mounted his own horse, took the man's reins, and started over the hill, Misha noticed that the prisoner was just a kid, fifteen at most. As they rode, he wondered whom the youth would be leaving behind and how they would get along without him and decided to question him.

152

"How did you become part of this gang? Don't you know you are murdering innocent people?"

"I had no choice. I was drafted at gunpoint. They said they would kill my parents and my siblings if I did not join them," he replied.

After cresting the hill, Misha had to make a decision. Should he kill him or let him go? How could he pull the trigger on this boy? He had to hurry, or soon someone would be checking on him. "Do you want to live?"

"Yes, yes, I do," answered the young man. "Please let me live," he pleaded.

"All right, I will untie you. You will crawl underneath these bushes." He pointed to a large overgrowth. "I will fire into the ground. You will lie there until pitch darkness. Then you run home. Do not let anyone see you, or I will be court-martialed."

"I will do exactly what you have instructed," the youth answered softly.

Misha unbound the young man's hands, and he dismounted and disappeared into the bushes like a scared rabbit. Misha then fired into the ground, took the other horse by the reins and galloped back to his squadron. He reported to his commanding officer that he had carried out his orders, and the regiment began following the fresh tracks of a large group of horses.

Anuta was sitting and milking her cow one late afternoon, when she felt a heavy fearful feeling come over her, just like on the day her husband was murdered. She jumped up so suddenly that she accidentally knocked over the pail and spilled the milk. No matter. She needed to go ring the bell to warn everyone. She had learned to trust such feelings. She ran outside to the bell and rang it as loudly as she could.

Moments later, people began coming out of their homes carrying their rifles, looking all around for the danger but saw none.

"Who rang the bell?" a voice called out.

"Muslims are coming, I know it. I can feel they are near," Anuta yelled back to the voice.

Alixey stepped outside with his rifle. He was standing quietly, listening for the sounds of approaching horses. He knew his daughter. She was feeling something real.

It was quiet. No birds were chirping. He was about to head back into the house when he thought he heard something. He froze. Standing very still, he heard what his daughter was feeling.

He stepped over to the bell and rang it again, yelling, "Horses approaching!" Better to be ready, even if it turned out to be nothing. He turned to Anuta and ordered her into the house to tell everyone to get down on the floor.

Anuta ran inside and yelled, "Everyone, get down!"

Alixey ran out onto the road with his loaded rifle to see if anyone else was out there and ready. He saw young men and women also armed. His heart was pounding. The thought of killing or of being killed terrified him. He had never before shot at another human being. But he would do it to defend his family. The dogs in the village started barking.

Suddenly someone shouted, "They are coming up on us from behind!"

Alixey ran to the corral behind the barn. He could see them now. Not friendly. They were the enemy. He leaned his rifle on the corral fence and prepared himself. He heard someone call out, "They are coming from the south!"

Someone else called, "They are also coming from the north!"

Trying hard to focus, Alixey thought to himself, *Is this the end of us?* Fear flooded his mind, heart and soul. He was tingling all over. His arms felt heavy. His mouth was dry. But he was going to take a stand and die if he had to.

Suddenly he heard the loud crack of a rifle and a bullet whistled past his right ear. They were shooting at him. He took aim and pulled the trigger. Crack! The man fell from his horse. By this time the air was filled with the sound of rifle volleys, smoke and the smell of gunpowder. Alixey quickly reloaded, took aim and shot again, killing another man. All of a sudden, splinters flew in all directions. Some hit him in the face and bounced off. The bullet had hit the fence. He reloaded and fired a third time.

"Soldiers are coming," someone yelled out an upstairs window.

Moments later the enemy were falling from their horses one right after another.

It was Misha and his platoon. They had followed the tracks until they led them to Chubaroyka.

Shots continued as the enemy was being wiped out. Misha was up on a grassy mound shooting at the invaders. A bullet hit the ground with a loud zing and spooked his horse, which reared up. As Misha yelled, "Wow!" a hot bullet flew into his mouth and out his right cheek, leaving part of it hanging. Blood was pouring down his chin. His horse was still on its hind feet. It spun around as a bullet hit him in the left shoulder, another in his left side. He fell to the ground and passed out.

The battle had been won. The enemy was defeated and not one villager had died. Seven soldiers were wounded, some worse than others.

19
Healings

Feta had finished her schooling and had been home for several months. While away, she had learned how to care for bullet wounds. The church was turned into a hospital, and Feta rode out to the meadows to gather the herbs she needed. They must be fresh so she could squeeze the juice into the wounds. She took charge, showing the women of the village what to do and how to do it. Some women tore up clean sheets for bandages as the wounded men lay on blankets on the floor, while Anuta, her mother and others tended to the wounded soldiers. The men— including the remaining soldiers—collected the bodies, loaded them on wagons, drove to an unclaimed meadow, dug graves and buried them. Before long all the wounded were bandaged and the soldiers were resting.

Misha's face had swollen, and he was in pain from the bullet that was lodged in his side. His shoulder was not as bad; the bullet went through it. The loose part of the cheek that lay against his face irritated him. He unraveled the bandage from his face and felt the loose piece, hanging by a mere string of skin. He pulled it off and threw it aside.

Anuta came over to him, got down on her knees, dripped more healing juice on his face and bandaged him again. He soon dropped off to sleep, but it was a restless one. From his ravings she learned he had a son named Ivan. He kept telling him that he was going to be all right and would soon be home again.

Most were flesh wounds where the bullet had gone clean through, but Misha's side had no exit wound; the bullet was still in it. Feta was an herbalist, not a doctor. She just kept dripping healing herb juice over the wounds and giving him healing teas to drink. In time the wounded men healed and left to go back to their posts. The soldiers were grateful for their care, and the villagers were grateful for their rescue.

Misha and another man were the last to leave. Misha's side had healed leaving a small entry wound. His shoulder was healing, but his arm had to be kept in a sling for a while. The right cheek was also healing, but it had a large scar, leaving him less good-looking than he had been.

Anuta nonetheless thought him tall, dark and handsome. He seemed to be kind and gentle and spoke like he was well educated. His voice was kind, his diction perfect, and he had a large vocabulary. But he had a secret.

Before he left, he asked if he could visit after his discharge, which he thought would be soon since the bullet was still in his side.

Anuta was taken by the way he carried himself. She asked about the son to whom he had been talking in his sleep, and when he informed her that he was a widower, she gave him permission to visit.

The Muslim fundamentalists had been defeated and again life in Chubaroyka became peaceful. Due to the bloody memories, several families decided they wanted to move. They found other villages to call home, sold their houses and properties, and left.

Misha bought one of the properties, and everyone was impressed by how well he remodeled his home. He started courting Anuta.

She saw how talented and hard-working he was. There was nothing he could not build or fix. She knew she would be well cared for. When he asked her to marry him, she accepted, even though she was still in love with Daniel. She might not get a chance again. Many men had been murdered, leaving four women to one man.

Alixey saw how diligent he was, and how gently he treated his daughter, so he gave his blessing.

A month later they were married and moved into his beautiful home. He had even doubled the size of the root cellars. He was good to her. He was up and gone working either out in the fields or in the barnyard before she woke up. He would come in for breakfast and go back to work until dinner. When she needed new shoes, he would make her an impressive pair. She was envied by many of the women.

After they were settled and got to know each other, he asked if it would be all right with her if his son, now seven years old, could come live with them.

Of course she agreed. She looked forward to being a mother again.

He hitched two horses to the wagon and left while Anuta stayed behind to care for the livestock. Misha was gone four days and finally returned with his young handsome son Ivan. He was fair-skinned, with dark brown hair, a round face and blue eyes, a good-looking boy who got second glances from the little girls.

Ivan did not know his father very well, having been only three years old when he was drafted into the military. Misha left his son with his sister Anna and came home for short visits. Ivan had not spent much time with his father, so he was shy around him on the trip home.

When Misha brought Ivan home, he had to get to know his stepmother, but he soon warmed up to her. He began calling her Mama from the first day. Ivan's mother had died six weeks after his birth and this broke Anuta's heart. She decided she would be a good mother to him.

Ivan grafted in very quickly and was a big help to both his parents. His father taught him to track and hunt wild game and to fish the rivers. Evenings he would hobble the horses and let them out to graze. In the morning he would go track them down and bring them back. He learned to care for the beehives and the livestock. He was very good at building things. He taught the dog to pull a little wagon that he built himself, and took turns riding in it with his friends. Anuta was impressed at all his abilities at such a young age.

There was talk of communism coming into their land. Chiang Kai-shek was running the country, but Mao Tse-tung was doing all he could to overthrow him. Many civilians took up arms and left for the battlefront to help their country. Mao passed a law: anyone aiding the resistance in any way would be executed.

Misha and Anuta were pro-Chiang Kai-shek and secretly sent food to the battlefront. No one in their village knew, not even Anuta's family, only the person who would show up in the middle of the night to collect the food knew.

Misha's three sisters and brother moved to Chubaroyka; their former village was no longer safe. There was a new lawlessness, and people were robbed or murdered senselessly. They felt it would be safer nearer their brother Misha. Anna, Irina and Ganya all married.

Maxim was only fourteen and lived with his sister Anna. He and his playmate Alexander were terrified when ordered to join

Mao's army. They were supporters of the freedom that they were currently enjoying and did not want to fight for Mao, but if they failed to report, they would be shot for treason. Before leaving, Maxim went to his brother to bid him farewell.

Misha advised him to flee. He had heard about a group of a hundred or more men who were planning to flee to India over the Himalayan Mountains, then through India to America. "Maxim, you are only fourteen. You are too young to be a soldier. Join that group; take your friend with you and flee. There is a country called America; I have heard it is a great country. There is freedom there, and it is a land of opportunity. Once you get there, maybe you can help me and my family to go there." His heart was aching, but he had to help his brother. "Do not say anything to your sisters. I think they are pro-Mao. I know how to contact the group. Your friend must not say a word to anyone, just flee." Misha might never see his little brother again; he might be shot for fleeing or freeze in the Himalayas. They gave each other a long tearful goodbye and hug. Misha quietly whispered the information into Maxim's ear. Before he left, Maxim promised that when he got to this America he would contact Misha and help him and his family to join him there.

Maxim went straight to Alexander's house to talk him into coming along. His friend, terrified of the battlefield,, was easily persuaded. Quietly, they contacted the refugees, now 120 strong, who accepted them into their fold, meeting them in an old abandoned house in the middle of the wilderness. The group had camels and horses prepared, and two nights later they left for the Himalayas.

Anna woke the next morning and found Maxim's empty bed. In a panic she ran to Misha's house and burst in without knocking, startling Misha and Anuta.

"Maxim is gone! His bed was empty when I woke this morning. Is he here with you?" she bellowed.

Misha and Anuta knew where he was but denied knowing anything.

It broke Misha's heart to see his sister so distraught but he was not sure he could trust her. Many families were divided by the new order that was flooding the land. Many people were turning in their family members for being disloyal. Anuta was eight months pregnant with their first. He could not risk telling Anna anything. It hurt him deeply when she left tearfully calling out Maxim's name.

Anuta tried to comfort Misha, but he drew into himself and stayed that way for weeks. She knew how much he was suffering. Suffering was no stranger to her. It had visited her many times. She just continued to love him. She knew that he was no fool and that he would eventually talk himself out of it.

One month later, Anuta gave birth to a little boy. Misha took one look at him and joy returned to his sadly broken heart. They decided on the name Vasili after Misha's grandfather.

Anuta recovered from the childbirth and was able to join her husband in the wheat field. They cut the wheat with scythes, tied the stalks in bundles and stood them with the stock pointed upward to dry. That night, the man who came to collect the food for the war front asked if they would turn their cellar into an underground hospital. It seemed the opposing side was becoming stronger, and the resistance was suffering more and more wounded.

Misha and Anuta were nervous about this. There was now a military post just outside the village. If they were found out, they would be executed. They talked it over while the man sat at their table and refreshed himself with the food set in front of him, and they decided to chance it. Freedom for their children was well worth the risk. They agreed, with the understanding that these wounded would only be brought in during the night and only one at a time. They also agreed that if caught, they and the wounded would tell the military that the man had stumbled onto their doorstep. They did not know who he was, but they were compelled by their Christian beliefs to help the man.

The next day a bed was set up in their root cellar with all the soldiers would need. It wasn't two days before the wounded started showing up. Between that and the wheat that needed to be brought in and winnowed, Misha and Anuta were very busy. They never shared any details with either of their families; it was all done in secret. Anuta was in a constant state of terror. Her reward was seeing the men leave again well enough to fight.

Many wounded men were brought to them. Some were injured too severely and died. It was very difficult for Misha and Anuta to see this, but it was something they knew would happen. One man had been wounded four different times. He would show up on their doorstep and they would tend to his bullet wounds. As soon as he was better, he would go back to the war front. Anuta asked him why he didn't just go home after being wounded so many times. He told her he was determined to keep communism out of China, even if it cost him his life. They got to know each other quite well and bonded in friendship. One sad day she heard that he had perished on the battlefield. Anuta mourned his death as a family member. She would never forget his sacrifice.

20

Vasili

Vasili, now nine months old, started to take his first steps. Anuta loved this child so much for his eagerness. He knew he was his mama's little man. He did not care if his legs were strong enough to carry him or how many times he had to get up off the floor. He was going to master this thing called walking. Every morning when she went to his crib, he was just patiently waiting for the chance to wake up and start the day. Every morning he greeted her with a great big smile. His big blue sparkly eyes melted her heart. He was becoming the image of his father, having his dark hair, though with curls like hers. His father was always out working before he woke up, but Ivan greeted him with great cheer when he returned for breakfast.

Misha and his sister Irina had several heated discussions about communism. Misha detested it and Irina welcomed it. This fragmented their relationship, so Misha knew he could not trust her; he became extra careful around her.

One night Irina was on her way out to the outhouse, when she saw someone bring a wounded man to her brother's home. She saw the door open; he was unloaded and taken straight inside as if expected. Later that day her husband advised her to turn him in. She got on her horse, rode out to the military post and informed them of her brother's activities. She then left the village for a few days so that she would not have to witness the consequences.

Misha and Anuta were immediately under suspicion but were unaware of all the eyes now watching them. That evening, they were quietly eating dinner when they heard footsteps on their roof. Misha knew they were in trouble. He jumped down into the root cellar and told the wounded man to come up and take a seat at the table. Anuta set a place for him as if he had been eating with them. Misha took the bed apart and hid everything that might look as if they were treating him. He then came up, closed the trap door and laid a rug over it. He needed to assess the situation. He told Anuta that he was going outside to see how many men were out there.

Anuta was weeping, knowing their situation was very serious. She ran and picked up Vasili, who had just been laid down for the night. Ivan also was in bed. She decided to let him sleep. Perhaps by some miracle they would just be questioned.

Misha stepped out the back door and called back to Anuta that he was going to the outhouse, and he'd be right back. He slipped into the shadows to observe what was going on around the house. He saw ten armed soldiers. Five were on the roof, and five were milling around the house trying to look in the windows, but the curtains were too good a barrier. He knew they all had to stick to the same story in order to get out of this alive.

Anuta was trying with all her might to keep her emotions in check. If she broke down , it would be the same as a signed confession. Suddenly the door was pushed open, and the soldiers piled into the house. Misha, seeing this, quickly rushed into the house.

"Well, hello there, brothers! What can we do for you tonight?" Misha said gently, trying to act surprised.

"You are under arrest," growled the one who seemed to be in charge.

"Why are we under arrest?" Misha asked the man.

"Do you have a sister named Irina?"

"Yes, I do."

"She tells us you are part of the resistance."

Misha acted even more surprised. "How are we part of the resistance?"

Before he got an answer, two soldiers grabbed the wounded man, dragged him outside and shot him.

Vasili was terrified by what had just occurred. He started shrieking. Anuta did her best, but he was inconsolable. He grabbed her with both hands and clung tightly. She could feel his body break out in a sweat. His little face was wet with tears and sweat and moisture was coming through his shirt. Terrified she might lose him like she lost Yoseph, she started weeping quietly as she held him tightly in her arms, but he continued to shriek.

Ivan heard the gunshot, got out of bed, ran to his father's side and wrapped his arms around his waist.

"My son, run to your Aunt Anna's house and stay there until I come and get you."

Ivan let go and took off running. His father watched as his bare feet ran out of the yard and into the darkness.

Misha was terrified that he might not ever see him or his wife or little Vasili after this night. He determined it was for a good cause. If any proof were found, they would not harm his wife. He would accept all the blame on himself and insist that he forced her to go along.

While they stood outside at gunpoint, four soldiers searched the house. They slammed things around. Occasionally Misha and

Anuta could hear them curse. Anuta knew God blinded their eyes and dulled their thoughts. No one moved the rug and pulled up the trap door to the root cellar. Had they searched there, they would have found what they sought.

The soldiers finally came out looking disappointed. They walked off a little way and whispered amongst themselves. Misha and Anuta tried to listen but could not make out what was said. Six men got up on their horses and rode off, uplifting Misha's and Anuta's spirits. But four men remained, causing the couple apprehension. What was going on? Neither of them could say a word, and it was too dark to communicate by eye contact. They waited, trembling.

The one in charge came up to Misha and informed him that he and his wife were going to be taken to different headquarters for questioning. If all checked out, they would be released.

Before he was finished, a man rode up with two riderless horses. Anuta begged them to let her leave her son with her parents, but her request was denied. It was starting to turn cold. She asked if she could at least get a blanket for Vasili. Again they denied her permission, but a man went in and brought one out. She handed Vasili to Misha and mounted the horse. Misha then handed their son up to her. She wrapped him up and got a good grip. A soldier was already mounted and waiting; he rode up, took the reins, and they rode off into the night.

For a few kilometers she knew where they were, but beyond that she was unfamiliar with the area. She decided to ask the man leading her horse. "How far are we going, sir?" she asked politely, fighting waves of terror.

"We are going to a post twenty kilometers from here," he curtly answered.

Little Vasili was asleep. All Anuta had at this moment was God, so she quietly prayed.

166

Then once again she asked, "Where are they taking my husband?"

"To another post not far from where I am taking you."

Once again Anuta started to pray for God's mercy and strength. After a long ride, they arrived at the post. The man dismounted, walked over to Anuta and took Vasili from her. She climbed down herself and took her son back.

The man took Anuta by the arm and jerked her in the direction they needed to go. To keep up the appearance of innocence, she cooperated. They walked to a dimly lit room with a table and three chairs. She was ordered to sit in one. As she sat down, the man yanked Vasili out of her arms, waking him. He started to cry. Anuta stood up and tearfully begged to have her baby back. Without a word the man stomped out of the room and slammed the door.

Over and over Anuta heard Vasili crying for her. She broke down into deep sobbing. His voice started to sound muffled and then went silent. She went to the door to see what was happening only to find she had been locked in. Pounding on the door brought no results, and she knew it was a ploy to break her. She sat and listened for his cry but there was none. *They had done something to him!* she thought and wept. Hours passed as she sat there listening for sounds but there were none, so she prayed.

Finally she heard men's voices on the other side of the door. Someone unlocked it, and in strode a tall dark-haired man with dead brown eyes. He sat in a chair opposite her and silently stared at her for a moment. Before he said a word, Anuta demanded that her son be returned to her at once.

He gave her a smug, arrogant smile, and replied, "You will get him back when you have answered all our questions."

"Where is he?" she demanded. "Why don't I hear him?"

"He is being taken care of in the building out back. Now answer all my questions, and you two can go."

"I want to see him first," she shouted, as she slammed the table with her fist.

His dead eyes were fixed on her. He acted like he did not hear a word and proceeded to question her. "Why was that wounded man in your house?"

"He knocked on our door. When my husband answered it, he was standing there all bloody. We could not send him away. So we let him come in. We did not know who he was or where he was from. We just did the Christian thing—you know—love your neighbor as yourself. We were going to feed him and take him where he needed to go."

The man sat there silently, continuing to stare at her. He was just trying to intimidate her. It wasn't working. She was no stranger to suffering, so she just sat quietly.

After a few moments, he stood up and told her he would be back after he talked to her husband. Before he left, Anuta asked for her son again.

"All right," he replied. "You can have him. Someone will bring him to you." Without another word, he left.

Anuta was finally feeling hopeful—she was getting her son back. She patiently sat and waited. Someone opened the door, and a man walked in carrying her son still wrapped in his blanket. He was quiet. *He must be sleeping,* she thought. Quickly getting up, she walked up and took him from the man. He felt limp as she laid him on the table. Before she unwrapped him, the door slammed shut again. Her heart was beating, her thoughts racing. Something was very wrong. When she unwrapped him, his eyes were open, and he was still and not breathing. She put her ear on his chest to listen for a heartbeat—only silence. He was dead.

She crumpled to the floor and wept deep bitter tears. After a good long cry she stood back up, leaned down and gave him a long goodbye kiss. She quietly spoke to her little man. "Now your suffering is over. Go be with your sisters Anya and Anya and your brother Yoseph. We will meet again someday." She broke down and began to weep again. She swept him up into her arms, wrapped the blanket around him, sat back down and just rocked his lifeless body.

Once again the door opened. The dead-eyed man walked in, still wearing his smug grin. "Did you get your son back?"

Anuta just nodded.

"Well, you may go. Your husband's story matches yours."

"Can I get a horse at least?" Anuta asked.

"No, no horse," was his answer. "You get home any way you want. Please go." He opened the door and stepped aside.

Anuta stood and walked out. She did not know which direction to go. She saw a little road and started down it. Her heart was so numb that she wanted to give up right there. But her family would not want that for her. Slowly she put one foot in front of the other. At last she could see a small cluster of houses, and she picked up her pace till she came to one. By the appearance of the house and barn, these people were wealthy. When a man answered her knock, Anuta broke into tears, explained why she needed his help and asked him to drive her home. The man seemed uncaring and told her to go away. Anuta, feeling completely defeated, turned and walked back to the road. After a few steps, her knees buckled and she fell face down in the dirt, still clutching Vasili's body. Through fresh tears she called out, "God, this is not Your fault. You are not to blame for any of this. You are a good God. You took care of my forefathers, and You will take care of me."

Just moments earlier in a nearby yard a little old man had had a strong sense to hitch his horses to his wagon. He did not know why, but the sense was stronger than his reasoning. He heard Anuta's crying out to God, looked out and saw her crumpled on the ground. He got in the wagon and drove out to her.

Anuta, still crying, did not hear him approach.

He climbed down and hurried over to her. "Young miss," he addressed her. At that moment he knew she was the reason the wagon needed to be ready. "Let me help you, young miss." He then gently helped her to her feet. "Let me take you where you need to go."

Anuta desperately needed to blow her nose but did not have a handkerchief so the man gave her his, then helped her get up into the wagon. After Anuta composed herself she thanked the man for his help. She told him where to go, and everything that had occurred at the military post. The man was filled with such compassion and felt it his privilege to help; so a weathered elderly man drove the wilted rose back to her village, neither one saying a word. She was exhausted from all that had taken place. Her family would be looking for her; by now Ivan must have said something to his Aunt Anna, and surely she had to have informed her parents. It seemed like forever before they reached the village. At her request he took her to her parents' home. She did not want to be alone; she wanted to be with her family.

As they pulled up to the house, Lara and Mark were in the yard. Immediately they ran into the house calling out that Anuta was home. Both her parents came out. They looked as if they had been weeping. Her father thanked the man for bringing her home and invited him in. He took little Vasili's body, handed it to Anya, and helped Anuta off the wagon.

"No, thank you," the man replied. "I need to get back to my wife." He turned the wagon and drove off.

Anuta's mother discovered that her grandson was dead and started lamenting. Anuta fell into her father's arms and wept. She told him about Misha, so he saddled two horses, one for himself and one for Misha and rode out to bring him home.

Anya laid little Vasili's body on a clothes chest in her bedroom and closed the door. She needed to start cooking for the funeral reception.

When Misha's sister Anna heard, she came to find her tearful sister-in-law sitting in her parents' family room by herself. Anna walked over and sat beside Anuta, and they both wept. Anna went next to where Vasili's body lay and continued to weep over him.

Alixey and Misha came home in the middle of the night. Misha went in to see his son's body. He immediately knew that the boy had been suffocated. Being in the military, he had had to suffocate a few men himself. He recognized the redness in the eyes, and knew it had been deliberate murder.

Misha built his son a little coffin and dug the grave himself. After the funeral he asked his wife to go stay with her parents for a few days, as he had to take care of a couple things. But what he really meant was that he had to take care of a couple of people. He understood war, but the murder of a child not even a year old was not something he would overlook. He had a surprise waiting for the two men, the one who had questioned her and the one who had led her horse away.

The first official lived in a small house behind the post where his wife had been questioned. He rode the twenty kilometers out to the post, a tiny building with just a small office and an interrogation room, and tied his horse just out of sight. Sneaking up to the building, he quietly freed the horses to prevent pursuit.

As the horses slowly wandered off, he lay down in the shadows and waited. With only one bullet, he could not afford to miss. After what seemed like hours, the man came out to use the outhouse. Misha carefully sighted, gently squeezed the trigger, the rifle fired and the man dropped. Misha quickly ran to his horse, mounted and galloped away.

Now for the other. Misha had decided—though his son would not approve—that since this official had murdered his son, he would not hesitate to kill someone else's son or daughter, and Misha was going to stop him. He rode home, unsaddled and hobbled the horse, then slunk out to where he could see the village post. Again when the opportunity arose, he set the horses free and waited patiently in the bushes. When at last the man stepped out with two men on either side of him, Misha knew he could not miss. He had to get this job done with one bullet. He took careful aim, squeezed the trigger and—Blam!—the rifle rang out. The man dropped. He quickly clambered out of the bushes and deliberately created tracks that led north of the village. Then, leaving no tracks, he carefully returned home and stashed his rifle.

Afterwards, he went to Irina's house. He thought about kicking in the door, but knocked instead. He gave her an ultimatum: "Be gone in one week, or the house catches on fire with you in it."

Irina knew her brother was not a man to threaten idly. He told her she was never to contact him or any other family member. If he found out that she had contacted anyone, he would hunt her down. She was dead to him and to everyone else. In less than one week she and her husband were packed, not knowing where to go but back to Russia.

Irina's husband, knowing Misha, was overcome by fear and hanged himself. However, Irina had created a reputation for herself, and she could not go to anyone for help. Anna's husband decided to help her. He dug a grave, built a coffin and buried the man, but no one attended the funeral. After several failed attempts to hire someone to drive her, Irina rode off in a wagon by herself.

21

Departures

Alixey and Anya had had enough of Chubaroyka. Too many memories of death and murders. They needed a new start. They'd been thinking about moving to Kalgatone, a village near the town of Kultza where they could sell their honey and wheat at bazaars held in the town square. There they would have the privacy of the village and the security of the nearby town.

When the news of Anuta's ordeal reached Tanya, she and Sergey came to visit with the intention of getting Anuta and Misha to move to Arsalon, only twenty-five kilometers southwest of Kalgatone.

When Tanya, Sergey and Dima arrived, Anuta met them with tears of joy. It was just like old times; they were together again.

Tanya could only stay a few days. Her neighbor was taking care of the livestock and milking the cows but had her own to care for, so would tire of it before long. So Tanya came out with it right away. "Anuta and Misha, Sergey and I are here to sway you to move to our village."

She did not have to try very hard.

Pulled from the Ashes: Departures

Misha had killed the two men who had murdered their son. He was a little concerned that he might be found out and arrested or executed. He lived by the rule of "an eye for an eye," but his wife might not see it the same way. Sparing her the worry, he never spoke a word to her about it. Without much persuasion, he and Anuta announced they were selling their house and property. The wheat had been harvested and was in the barn, so he had time to go and build them a home in Arsalon. First, though, they needed to go together and choose property.

Anuta would be glad to be living close to Tanya again, but at the same time sad. Her parents would be a distance away. They had never been so far apart, but Misha assured her that they would visit often.

Misha went and talked to Anna, and informed her of his plan. He also confessed that Maxim was on his way to America, by way of the Himalayan Mountains and through India. He asked her to stay put until she heard from him. Then she was to bring him the letter and follow them to Arsalon.

Anna was relieved to hear about Maxim and where he was. She had been thinking he might have been killed. At the same time she was angry at Misha for advising him to travel such a dangerous route. Those mountains were very unforgiving. The winds were cold and strong; they could blow the clothes off your back. Misha assured her that Maxim would be fine, and when he told her Alexander had gone with Maxim, she settled down.

Anuta and Misha followed Tanya and her husband to their new village. Anuta fell in love with it. It had tall hills on three sides and a lazy river running through it. She had never seen so many wild berries, apples and apricots. She saw the wild onions, the rhubarb, the strawberries. They found a piece of property, mere feet from the river, that would be just right and bought it.

Misha drove Anuta home, then came back and started building. The new neighbors and Sergey helped. Some cut down trees, others stripped them. By fall a large cabin stood empty and waiting for its occupants. The two-room cabin, with a dirt floor as smooth as glass, had no separate bedrooms. The kitchen was on one side, the bed on the other. Boards in the rafters with a rail across made a sleeping loft for Ivan. One window over the dining table opened inward for ventilation; a cast iron cook stove and a brick baking oven along the same wall served as a bed. The pantry was a separate room. It was necessary to walk through it to reach the front door. In the winter it would be a cold room for storing milk, eggs and left-overs. To live there permanently was not Misha's intention; he was hoping to someday move to America. But for now this home would be warm and safe.

The barn, a large two-story building, was built from sawn logs. The top half was for storing hay, the bottom for grain, along with areas for livestock and for storing the wagon and sleigh. Misha was a man who could do anything. His grandfather, who invented the steam locomotive in Russia, had taught Misha the art of smithing. So Misha put in an area where he could make horseshoes to sell.

He built a fence around the corral and another around the house. People had to have dogs for hunting and protection, but he did not want to keep his tied up all the time. This way they had a fenced-in area in which to run. The chicken coop was outside the fence so the dog could not get to it.

Ducks, geese and chickens were necessary, but Anuta loved them and always wanted large flocks, not just a few of them. She loved the sounds that they made and the way the ducks and geese swam on the water. A very clean person, she kept her home spotless and the chicken coop well cared for.

176

Arsalon had a common garden area near one edge, right along the river. Misha dug a ditch from the garden to the river; all the women of the village had to do was to pull up a sluice, and the river water would trickle all through the garden.

At last all was finished: the house, the barn and the chicken coop. The neighbors welcomed Misha to use their bath house, so he did not build one of his own. He went home and packed up. Several neighbors offered their wagons and help. Alixey and Anya also helped.

First everything was moved from one house to the other, and then the livestock were driven to their new grazing area. The chickens, ducks and geese were all caught during the night and their feet hobbled so they would not hurt themselves or others when transported. The beehives were also covered with canvas in the dark after the bees went in for the night and driven to their new wildflower fields.

During the move Misha's sister Ganya received word that Irina had been so grief-stricken by what she had done that she lost the sight in one eye. Ganya felt compassion for her and was going back to Russia to be near her.

Misha knew that once she left they would never see each other again. He would never go back to Russia, and she would never be allowed to leave. After a long goodbye Misha stepped back and took a long look at her to imprint her face in his memory: her blonde hair and brown eyes, the round face that reminded him of his mother. Then he turned and walked out the door. He hoped she would contact Anna and that Anna would forward the message to him. He wanted to keep in touch with Ganya.

Before approaching the wagon where his Anuta was waiting, he wiped his tears. He needed to maintain an appearance of strength for her. He climbed on the wagon, and they drove off to their new home.

Ivan would miss his Aunt Anna, but he knew his father would take them back for visits.

Sometime later, Alixey and Anya bought a little farm in Kalgatone to be nearer the family.

22

Arsalon

Anuta and Misha settled into their cozy new home where they spent the first winter. When the snow was melting and patches of new grass could be seen, the neighbors warned them that any day now a tribe of nomads, who sometimes stopped nearby if the snow melt was too slow, would be driving their sheep and camels through to meadows in the high hills. Horses were to be corralled until the camels were gone lest they be trampled by the nasty beasts. A friendly people whose children played with the village children, the nomads sometimes stopped and traded gold for honey and bread from the villagers.

Misha and Anuta had plenty of honey because of Misha's skills with his bees, and Anuta was a master at baking; so they watched for the nomads. They would need the gold to pay for their trip to America if they were ever privileged enough to go.

Two weeks went by with no sign. Then a young man named Roman rode through the village on his Altai horse, shouting that the nomads and their herds were drawing near. Misha got the honey ready. Anuta made batches of bread dough in all the pots and pans that she could find. Her big brick oven could bake eight loaves all at once.

The camels were curious animals that would go off exploring if the owner was not watching. Sometimes they rushed strangers, so people kept a close eye on their children. Anyone new to the village was instructed to head to a river and along the bank if a camel gave chase. Camels have smooth skin on the soles of their feet; therefore they would have no traction on the smooth river bank and would slip and fall, giving a person a chance to get away. If they got mad, they would spit or butt with their heads. The really mean ones had to wear bells; if a ringing was heard, it meant get out of sight until the sound was gone. People who did not follow these rules were sometimes killed by these nasty animals.

Misha had been around camels; the military used them to carry their machine guns. He was unafraid of them and somehow they knew this. He told his wife the story of a camel that was in his charge that developed blisters on the soles of its feet from the rough rocky terrain that they were crossing. Bark, as pliable and as tough as leather, was stripped from a tree and sewn with needle and thread onto the soles of the camel's feet. They ran the needle through the callused part of its feet and called it shoeing the camel.

Anuta laughed after hearing this story. Leave it up to Misha to come up with something like that, she thought. He truly was a smart and educated individual. There was nothing he could not do. If he were stumped, it would only be for a moment. He could figure out anything or anyone. She knew she had made a good decision when she married him, but she never forgot her Daniel.

Anuta baked thirty loaves of bread and set them on the table. Before long the village was full of nomads. They drove their camels up a hill a short distance from the village, then returned for honey and bread from anyone who would sell it. Misha went out to the street and called out to the crowd. "Honey! Bread!" They took no time in circling him. He asked them to form a line in front of the window, came back inside, opened the window, took their gold and handed them bread and honey. It wasn't long before everything was sold out.

Anuta and Misha knew communism would come to the village before long; they had to hide this gold in case they were searched. Anuta came up with an idea: hide it in the chicken coop under the droppings. What clean self-respecting person would search a pile of chicken manure? Every time gold was acquired, there it went.

One morning Anuta went to milk the cow and the smells nauseated her. She knew exactly what was happening. She had buried every child she had had and thought of them every day. *Would this one live?* she wondered. After a long and difficult pregnancy, she gave birth to Makar. He had a full head of black hair. He was perfect and took to suckling as soon as he was handed to her. After holding him for a moment, she started to pray. "God, please, can I please raise this one? I'm so tired of having to go to the cemetery."

Misha was ecstatic; once again he had a son. He vowed to protect both his wife and son even at the cost of his own life.

Makar started to walk at nine months; he feared nothing. By his second birthday, his black hair had fallen out, and he was blond-haired and blue-eyed, the joy of his parents' lives.

Then his sister came along, born with a full head of brown hair. Misha took one look at her, and in a strange voice, swore he would kill her. Anuta was shocked. Why would he say that? She was a beautiful little girl. She tearfully questioned him about what he had said. He swore he didn't remember saying such a thing, but when the midwife, Tanya and other attending women told him they also had heard it, he left the house very suddenly. He feared his secret would be exposed.

Anuta was in tears and confused. Misha wasn't going to help her pick a name, so she named her Anisya. Misha later returned but kept his distance. There was something about this little girl that terrified him.

Anuta's parents and siblings had moved to Kalgatone. She wrote her parents a letter asking them to visit; they arrived a few weeks later. Anya took one look at Anisya and told Anuta the name was all wrong for her. She was too quiet to have that name. She looked like a Julia, meaning the beautiful one. So Julia became the name of the little girl.

Anya and Alixey noticed how Misha avoided her. Becoming suspicious, they started watching his every move. They noticed that three nights in a row he went out to the barn, always at the same time.

On the fourth night Alixey decided to follow him. As Misha walked into the barn and closed the door behind him, Alixey followed, quietly slipped in and watched as Misha walked to the back of the barn to a small box from which he took out a old worn black book. When he opened it, the pages became illuminated with an eerie light. Misha then proceeded to speak strange words. It sounded as if he were reading from the strange book. Alixey knew then why he disliked his daughter. Misha was practicing witchcraft. That explained it all. The spirit in Misha was afraid of the spirit in his little girl. Alixey quietly slipped out and quickly went back into the house to talk to his daughter before Misha returned. He reported to the women what he had just seen. They were shocked. Anuta had never suspected. Alixey advised Anuta to keep an eye on her little Julia; she was born for a purpose, and the spirit in Misha knew it, and would try to destroy her.

A few days later Anuta's parents left for home. She decided that since God gave Julia to her for a purpose, she would pay

182

extra attention to her. But Anuta did not know that Misha had dedicated Makar to Satan, and now it was his daughter's turn.

One early morning Misha pretended to be asleep. Anuta had to go to the outhouse. When she left, Misha quickly got out of bed, picked up Julia, waved her in the air and chanted over her. He dedicated her to Satan. He then laid her back down and went back to bed himself. When Anuta returned, everything seemed fine, so she started her morning routine. She started breakfast and went to milk the cow. Misha felt the threat was gone and things would return to normal. But they didn't, the spirit within her remained.

Julia started filling out. Her hair was curly, her eyes big, blue and shiny. She had a round face and was looking more and more like her father. In contrast to her brother, she was fifteen months old before she took her first step, but as soon as her legs became strong enough for walking, she began running and was unstoppable.

Makar frequently developed high fevers and would stay in bed for days. Julia never got sick. She started talking before she was two. A typical female, she liked to talk.

Two days after her second birthday, Anuta and Misha had another little blond-haired boy whom they named Petro after Anuta's uncle. He looked like Julia and his father and walked at nine months like Makar had.

When Petro turned two, Anuta gave birth to yet another little boy, Oseph, but two weeks later he died in his sleep. Tearfully they buried him. Anuta was beside herself and fell into a deep, deep sadness. Petro tried to get affection from her but was pushed aside. Anuta felt she had been spent and had no more love to give.

Julia

23

Darkness

One night when Julia was sleeping, she was awakened by a sense that an evil presence was approaching. She did not know what to call this evil, but she knew it was coming. A moonlit night, there was a faint light in the cabin. Suddenly a tall black figure with red eyes walked through the closed door. About seven feet tall, with the head of a buffalo and the figure of a man, it had hands and fingers, but its legs had hooves where the feet should be. It walked up and bent down over her. She tried to push it away, but it overpowered her and threw her around in her bed. She was so overcome with fear, her body went limp. This thing then pinned her down to the bed with his large ugly head and held her there.

She was overpowered by this thing. She tried to call out, but no sound came out. She wet herself and the bed. Finally it vanished. She did not sleep a wink the rest of the night. If this thing could walk through a closed door, what would stop it from returning?

Finally it was full daylight. Julia's straw mattress needed to be dried out. Her mother noticed that the back of her slip was wet and pulled it off, scolding her, and asked Ivan to take the mattress outside and drape it over the fence to dry in the sun. Julia was exhausted. Anuta took one look at her and again started scolding her for looking so tired. Julia knew how sad and broken her mother always seemed, so she kept everything to herself. She certainly could not tell her father; he barely tolerated her as it was. She tried to function through the rest of the day as well as she could. There were many children to play with, so she ran off with some of her friends and played at the riverbank most of the day. She never said a word to anyone about that night, though she was concerned about the upcoming evening.

That night when everyone went to bed, she also had to; the lantern was put out and the cabin was dark. Once again, with everyone asleep but her, she felt the evil approaching. Before long, by the moonlight she watched it walk through the closed door and do the same as the night before. Again she wet herself and the bed, but this time she was exhausted and fell asleep regardless.

In the morning she was again scolded, and her mattress was taken outside to dry. That day her parents and brothers went next door to visit Tanya and Sergey. Julia was grounded for wetting the bed. She stayed home and quietly sat on the floor and played with wooden toys. She heard the door open and close and turned to see who it was. It was a man she had seen around the village, but she did not know his name. He walked over to her and, without saying a word, grabbed her and threw her on the bed. When he tried to rip off her underpants, she tried to scream and fight him. He cupped his hand over her mouth, overpowered and raped her. When he was done, he warned her not to tell anyone, or he would kill her. Wordlessly, he left.

She knew this would be another secret that she would have to carry. Julia climbed off the bed, went to the river and cleaned herself up; she hoped to get back to the house before her family returned. She sat on her bed, put her arms around herself and started rocking and crying; she felt as if she were unraveling one thread at a time. She felt so dirty and unworthy, completely alone in the world, with no one with whom she could talk. Her mother was always so sad and her father seemed to be angry at her. The evil monster came back three to four times a week. She kept the secret and continued to wet the bed.

Anuta finally noticed that her little girl was suffering. She thought it was a physical problem and packed up all three children into the wagon and headed to see her mother. Perhaps Feta knew of an herbal mixture that might help.

Anuta was only six kilometers from the village when she heard a bell ringing; a mean-spirited camel was close by. She drove the horses to a tall haystack and threw the children up onto it. Holding the reins, she climbed up herself. The ringing got louder and closer. Before long a camel appeared and ran up to the haystack. Anuta started praying out loud, asking God to help. All three children were terrified and crying. The camel ran up to the horses and tried to pick a fight with them. One horse reared up on its hind feet and kicked the camel and it ran off. Gradually the sound faded away to nothing.

"Quickly, children, get back in the wagon," Anuta whispered.

Makar jumped from the top of the stack and into the wagon. Julia slipped and fell to the ground. Anuta helped her up on her feet and then into the wagon. Petro climbed down and onto the wagon like a little man. Anuta climbed up, snapped the reins, and away they went. Anuta kept snapping them until they were traveling at high speed. She did not want the camel to catch up with them if he was still anywhere around. When she was sure they were safe, she slowed down and the rest of the trip was quite pleasant. They saw rabbits scurry away from the road. They saw pheasants fly off and all sorts of other wildlife.

Alixey and Anya were glad to see them. Feta was now married to a young man named Georgiy. He was a little younger than she, but he loved her and had pursued her for a long time. He himself was a very handsome man with the sweetest blue eyes and black hair. Six feet tall, he towered over Feta, who was barely five feet. Natasha and Mark had also married, but they lived with their spouses' families. Katiya was only fourteen. Beautiful but a little wild, she scared guys off. They wanted quiet gentle women, and she was neither.

When Anuta climbed down from the wagon and helped the children down, her father took the horses by the reins and led them behind the house to the barn. He unhitched them and let them loose in the corral.

Makar and Julia met two of their cousins, Katya and Afonase, Lara and Natasha's children. They ran off to play and were taken into town. They saw houses that were close together and roads that were graveled. They went to a bazaar and bought pieces of pine tree pitch that was used as chewing gum and dried fruit. These were things they had not tasted before, and they truly enjoyed them.

When they returned home, Julia was given a large bottle of some cold herb tea and was ordered to drink it, so without protest she guzzled it. Afterward she asked about the purpose of that tea. Feta told her it was going to make her feel better. Julia thought it would take the fear and the heartache away. But it didn't, it was still there. She thought about telling Feta about everything that had happened to her but decided against it. She was afraid Feta would judge her unclean, as she deemed herself.

The next morning their grandmother made lovely hot oatmeal for breakfast. She set a bowl in front of all the children.

Then she added a spoonful of butter to each bowl and told everyone to mix it in. The oatmeal was so tasty they could not stop eating it. Anuta did not have oats in the village so her children never had eaten any before. They had soup for almost every meal, except on holidays. They ate stews and roasts. Anuta was good at baking and made lots of pastries.

The visit over, Anuta's father hitched the horses to the wagon and brought it up front. Anuta wanted to stay longer but had to get home and do needed chores. Misha did not milk cows, so Tanya was doing it for her, although she was caring for her own four-year-old and was expecting again. The trip home was quiet; the camel must have moved on.

Misha was glad to see his family return. He had supper in the oven, a young wild pig. He had gone out with Tuzik, the dog. Tuzik cornered it, and Misha shot it.

The next day Julia ran out to play, but no one was outside, so she decided to take a stroll in the garden. She wanted some yummy peas. Setting out in that direction, she was walking quietly, humming to herself, when suddenly a large cobra raised its hooded head out of a clump of grass. Julia wasn't worried about it. Snakes were frequently seen and usually scurried off.

A voice told her to look behind her. She did, and the snake was following close behind. Julia started to run and the snake sped up. Now Julia was panicking. Ahead was a wooden fence. She was sure that once she climbed over it the snake would not be able to follow, so up over the fence she went; so did the snake. Now she was terrified and crying. The voice instructed her to double back and head home. Julia did so, and the snake followed.

Julia's cousin Dima was in his yard splitting firewood for the coming winter when an audible voice told him to go to the garden. He lowered his ax and looked around to see who had spoken, but he didn't see anyone, so he went back to chopping.

Again he heard the voice telling him to go to the garden. This time he knew something was up. He dropped the ax and walked toward the garden. It wasn't long before he saw his little cousin running toward him and screaming.

"What's going on, Julia?" he called out to her.

"A big snake is chasing me," she called back.

He picked up several large stones, and told her to veer off to the right. She did, and Dima struck the snake and incapacitated it. He then told her to go home; he was going to kill the snake.

Julia was out of breath from all the running, so she walked slowly. As she started down a gentle hill, she saw five demons sitting on either side of the trail. Something told her not to make eye contact and to walk between them. So she hung her head and did just that. When they were far behind her, she was instructed not to look back. She did not know who was talking to her, but it made her feel good, so she asked why they were there. Again the voice talked to her and told her that they were there to witness the kill (her death). She came home deeply shaken, crawled onto her bed and went to sleep.

Later that afternoon Dima came over and told Anuta what had happened. It saddened her that her daughter never said a word. Had she done something to alienate her? Why was she carrying this burden on her own? She decided to go talk to Misha; he was doing something in the barn. She was deep in thought about the suffering Julia was going through. She walked into the barn, seeing him as she started walking toward him. As she came close, she realized he was chanting something. As far as she could tell, it was inhuman, and the voice was different, coarse and deep. Terrified, she quietly walked out backwards. She went back into the house and started praying. It took a while before she stopped shaking. She wanted out of the marriage, but she had three children and recently had discovered she was pregnant again.

The children needed him—Makar and Petro worshiped him. She would not be able to survive on her own. So she decided to pin him down and find out exactly what it was that he was doing. Makar and Petro were out fishing with Ivan, so this would be a good time to talk.

She waited. Finally she heard his normal voice talking to the dog. She hurried outside to catch him before he got busy doing something in the garden.

"Misha, may I talk to you in the barn, please?" she asked him as she opened the barn door. She stepped in, and he followed. Anuta was shaking inside; her heart was racing, and her mouth was dry. But she needed answers.

"What do you need?" Misha asked in a gentle voice.

"I heard you chanting a little while ago. It wasn't even your voice, and it wasn't a human language. What are you up to? I need the truth, or the children and I are leaving."

Misha hung his head, sighed and began explaining. "When I was a young boy, my mother introduced me to witchcraft. She told me I would have many powers and I would be respected by many. So I joined, after a horrible ritual. I got so deep into it I eventually became a warlock. Now I am a prisoner. I have to give Satan whatever he requires, or he will kill me. But I only practice white magic."

"I don't want to know anything about white or black," Anuta snapped back. "Could this be the reason you are distant from our daughter?"

"I love her very much. I adore everything about her. But at the same time I am terrified of her," he answered.

"Will you cause her any harm?" Anuta demanded to know.

"Never," Misha answered.

"Then why don't you just quit?" Anuta asked.

"There is no quitting. I signed something with my own blood. Only death can set me free."

Anuta felt so hopeless. This was a good man standing before her. How could he have gotten into such filth? She had to ask him one more question—to which she did not want to hear the answer; she had to know where the children stood in this whole matter. "Have you chanted over the children?"

"I dedicated them to Satan."

"Why?" she tearfully cried out as she raised her fists and started pounding on his chest.

Misha grabbed her hands. He was sorry he hurt them but he needed to explain it to her. "Satan demanded it. He told me he would kill all of us if I didn't."

"Well, mister, my God is more powerful than yours and we'll see who wins." She pushed him aside and ran back into the house. She slammed the door, stood before the icons and begged God to rescue their family.

Misha came in after her to try to comfort her. He came in to see this wilted rose begging her God for help. He stood silently out of respect for her. When she quieted down, Misha walked up to her, took her in his arms and just held her. Neither one said a word. He knew they were on opposite sides of the fence. He had to ask her to keep this secret for the children's sake. If anyone found out, they would be shunned.

Later that night he talked to her. She agreed to keep his secret on one condition: he had to promise never to do any more of his chanting on their property. He had to go out into the woods to some unowned place where no one lived. She did not want this blackness touching anyone else.

The next morning Julia was out in her yard playing with her friend Irina, and they saw Irina's brother Tomas coming back from a trip to Kultza, the little town south of Kalgatone, where he had gone to buy some fancy material for a dress for his mother. When another man came over to him to ask about his trip, Tomas told him about the black man whom he saw there.

Julia and Irina were two girls with wild imaginations. They had never heard of such a thing; they thought people were only white. So they went down to the river to ponder this.

"The world must have other kinds of people besides us," Irina told Julia.

They decided to cause a riot in the village. They would undress, smear mud all over themselves, walk through the center of the village, and laugh as everyone ran for the hills. No one would know they were naked because they would be black. After they both were smeared with mud, including their faces, off to the center of the village they went and started walking. What happened next caught them by surprise. They were at the opposite side of the village from their clothes. The sun was warm, as was their skin, so all the mud dried and fell off, and they had a long naked walk through the village. People in their yards called them by their names and scolded them. The girls were shocked that anyone knew who they were. After all, their faces were covered with mud. Well, the news got back to their parents much faster than the girls into their clothes. They jumped into the river and washed off, laughing.

"Any moment now," Irina told Julia, "People are going to start running."

Well, no one did and when Julia got home at the end of the day, her father gave her a good spanking; first, for their motive, then for parading naked through the village.

The next day they were out to play again when they saw a woman place a baking sheet of cottage cheese rounds on the roof of her house. When dried, these were a tasty treat! So the girls hid out in the bushes. After a little while, when they were sure the treats were dry enough, they climbed on the roof and took them. The woman heard them and came out to see what was happening. Seeing the girls, she stepped back inside and appeared again with a long switch. Irina and Julia jumped to the ground, still hanging on to the treats. They started to run, and the woman gave chase. She chased them quite a long way before giving up. The girls ducked into a bath house and ate every tasty soggy round. Later that day they snuck back to the house and returned the baking sheet.

The women knew who the girls were and reported this to their parents. When Julia returned home, she was spanked again. That day she decided she did not like to be spanked. From that time forward she turned over a new leaf. Her mother seemed to be crying a lot, and Julia was not going to be the cause of it. From then on it was mud pies at the river bank.

24
The Letter

Misha's sister Anna received a letter from their brother
Maxim. The return address was Congers, New York, USA. It was
addressed to Misha. Anna wasted no time. She mounted her
horse and off she went to deliver it to Misha; she could not wait to
hear what Maxim had written them. After a long ride she reached
the village. She stopped to ask someone where her brother lived,
and they pointed out his house to her.

When she rode into the barnyard, Misha was repairing a
fence that someone's bull had knocked down to get to his cow.
Anna called out to him, climbed off the horse and pulled the letter
from her saddle bag. Misha rushed over to her and greeted her
with a hug.

Anuta heard the voices and, recognizing Anna's voice, she
stepped out to see if it was truly she. "Anna!" she called out,
"Welcome! Please come in."

All three went into the house.

Misha's hands started shaking as he saw the return address.
He carefully unsealed it and started to read it aloud. It said:

Pulled from the Ashes: The Letter

Greetings, my dear brother and sisters. I have finally made it to America. It is just as you said it would be, a land of opportunity. I have a job as a mason. I build things out of bricks and rocks. We ride around in cars and I don't have to go kill anything for dinner. I just go to the store and buy my food in packages or in cans or jars.

Everyone here says please and thank you. No one walks around with guns. They have people called policemen. They keep the peace and get paid to do it.

Now let me tell you about my trip here. When Alexander and I set out, there were over one hundred twenty-five people. The first day after we set out, I was sitting on my horse when a bullet whistled past my ear and the sound knocked me to the ground. They shot at me several more times. Thank God they missed. My horse grabbed my belt with her teeth and ran off, dragging me like a mother cat carries her kittens. Alexander followed on his horse. That was the only time we were shot at.

Later we stopped in a village to spend the night. Someone stole my horse.

The trip was beyond brutal. Along the way, Alexander's horse died and someone stole the gold cross that Tsar Nicholas awarded our father for his bravery. Many people died along the way; some starved, others froze to death. Alexander and I slept under the same bearskin blanket to stay warm. We searched everyone that died, but none of them had the cross. Only twenty of us made it to India alive. We did not have the strength or means to bury anyone. We kept moving, fearing pursuit. We slept just enough to keep from losing our minds. I know the gold cross was in the possession of one of those men. I can even pin it down to one, who will not explain how he bought a big house and a business. But we will let him be judged by God.

Now, my brother, please let me know if you are still living in the same area. Write me at the address I have written at the bottom of this letter. My boss says he will sponsor you and your family. You will have a job here for the rest of your life.

Love, Maxim

P.S. I have a girlfriend. You will like her. May only good things come your way.

The letter was dated three years back. After Misha finished reading the letter, he folded it up and put it away.

No one spoke. They just sat in silence trying to adjust to the idea that they now had a relative living in America. After a while Misha asked Anna if she would move to America.

She shook her head. "I can't. My husband has joined the communist party. I will not tell him about this letter. But you, my brother, work as hard as you can to get over there. Go in peace, my brother." She stood up and told Misha and Anuta she had to go. "I must get back before dark. I told my husband you were sick and I had to go see you. So if your paths cross, please tell him the same."

Misha nodded his head. He knew that this was probably the last time he would ever see her. But that was the price he had to pay for wanting freedom for his children.

The following Sunday Misha was sitting under a shade tree with his friends. He felt so proud of what his brother had accomplished. He pulled the letter out and read it to them, not knowing that one envious man would report him to the military post, now located directly across from Misha's house.

Anuta and the commander's wife had become close friends, and she frequently reported to Anuta what was being planned. One morning she went to Anuta's and warned her that everyone's rifles and ammunition would be confiscated. To avoid suspicion from her husband, she took a loaf of bread from Anuta's table and told her that her husband thought she was there for that purpose. She left without another word.

That night Misha and his sons took apart a small woodpile, wrapped the rifle and ammunition, dug a shallow trench, laid them in it and piled the wood over it. Another old rifle that misfired most of the time they hung on the gun rack, and it was that rifle that was taken.

The day after Misha read the letter to his friends, this woman came over again, this time in tears. She told them about the letter and how her husband knew about it. They were going to confiscate it, and Misha would be arrested. She wiped her tears, took a loaf and left.

Anuta quickly took the letter and copied the return address onto another piece of paper and laid the letter on the table. Not an hour later their yard was full of soldiers, who stormed the house, grabbed the letter and announced that Misha was under arrest. Anuta begged for forgiveness. She followed her husband outside. They brought him a horse and tied his hands behind his back. Anuta was frantic and screamed even louder.

Tanya heard the screaming and stepped out to see what was happening. She watched as Misha was hoisted onto the horse.

The commander had remounted. Anuta tearfully ran up to him and begged him not to take her husband. This man kicked her as hard as he could, and she fell over backwards.

Tanya had seen enough. She ran over to the man, grabbed him, lifted him up off his horse and over her head and slammed him to the ground as hard as she could, knocking the wind out of him.

"Compliments of a hard working woman," she shouted as she stood over him. She then turned to her sister and helped her up.

After he caught his breath the man got up. He was hunched over, holding his back. The rest of the men backed away. One man said just above a whisper, "Wow! Hercules woman!"

Anuta was terrified and certain that she or her sister would be arrested. But the man just slowly remounted and took the reins of Misha's horse.

Fifteen-year-old Ivan came home just in time to see them lead his father away. He called out. His father called back to him and told him to take care of the family. Ivan called back, "Papa, you can count on me!"

Julia had been playing by the river with her friends. When she heard the commotion and Ivan calling, she walked up to see what was happening. To see her father being led away on a horse with his arms tied behind his back hurt her so deeply that she never spoke about it. She saw her mother's tears and heard her cries and silently made her mother a promise never to misbehave or cause her any worry. She would do everything that she was told to the best of her ability.

The next day Anuta was sitting at the table combing her long blonde hair. Her children were gathered around her to comfort her—she had been crying non-stop ever since their father had been taken from them—when suddenly she fell silent. Her arms dropped to her sides and her hairbrush fell with a clatter. Silently she crumbled to the floor, and all four children screamed and called for her. Makar realized she had fainted. He gently tapped her cheeks and quietly called to her. Everyone watched breathlessly for a few moments until she opened her eyes. The children helped her up, and she sat back up on the chair, knowing she had to make some choices. She decided she must toughen up if they were going to come through this in one piece.

The next day she went to the military post to find out where her husband had been taken. She went to see him to find out what he thought she should do. Misha told her he wanted her to write a letter to Maxim and inform him of their situation.

After she got home she wrote a desperate letter; she told Ivan to sneak out to his Aunt Anna's village and to ask her to send it. They were being closely watched where they were; no way was the letter going to leave this place.

Ivan mounted his horse and quietly slipped away. He was gone for over a day. When a man showed up looking for him, Anuta told him that he had gone to visit his father.

When Ivan came home the next day, he was arrested and questioned. He said that he went to see his father but that a camel had chased him and in order to escape from the dangerous animal, he rode into the woods, went in the wrong direction and got lost; it had taken him till then to get home. The interrogator did not believe him and placed him in a concentration camp, not wanting him to help his father's family in any way, but he did not know this young man—Ivan had had to live by his wits for a long time and had learned a few tricks. Ivan did not doubt that he could figure out a way to sneak out and help his stepmother.

Several days later he was working in the fields, when he spotted a wild beehive in a hollow tree. He asked to be excused to relieve himself in the bushes but went directly to the beehive and stirred up the bees. After being stung several times, he went back to the field. Someone saw the raised welts on his body. Thinking it might be smallpox, the officials quarantined him to a secluded little cottage. He knew they would not be checking up on him, so he snuck out, crawled under the fence and ran home. His body ached from the stings, but that was unimportant at the time.

When he got home, he and his stepmother took the woodpile apart. He took the rifle and went hunting. After a few hours, he brought home a deer. They quickly hid the rifle back under the woodpile and he stole back to the concentration camp.

After carefully monitoring the routines of the guards, Ivan was often able, always at night, to slink out unseen and hunt, calculating how long the meat would last before he would need to do it again. Sometimes he brought back deer, other times wild geese. He would return to his prison unnoticed, and then work in the fields all the next day.

Anuta gave birth to Katiya, a quiet little girl with a full head of blonde hair, deep blue eyes and a soft feminine cry. She was so happy holding the little doll who, as the weeks went by, looked more and more like her Anya who died from cholera.

Anuta and the children lived on what Ivan brought home and on the vegetables from the garden. Then one day the villagers received notice that no one was to take anything from any garden, or harvest any wheat. It now belonged to the government. Everyone was to go to headquarters at the concentration camp where Ivan was being held and get a ration.

Anuta got on her horse with little Katiya and headed out there. She had to cross the Kosh River over the two logs, side by side, that served as a bridge and was terrified of its rapid current, although she had successfully crossed it several times before. Holding her baby tightly, she nudged her horse and it started across. Just before reaching the other side, the horse lost its footing and lunged forward. Katiya slipped out of Anuta's arms, fell face down into the river and floated downstream with the rapid current. Anuta leapt off the horse and jumped into the river after her baby, not caring that she could not swim. That did not matter now; she had to get her baby back. She kicked her legs and pulled herself along the bottom with her hands, caught up to the baby and grabbed her. It felt almost as if someone had handed the baby to her. She quickly crawled over to the shore, grabbed her baby by the legs and held her upside down. Katiya hung limp as the water drained from her mouth. Anuta turned her right side up. When Katiya gasped and started to cry, Anuta joined her. Sitting on the river bank, she was overcome by the thought that she could have lost her baby. A weakness welled up inside her, so she just sat and rocked the baby as she wept while her horse grazed close by.

She prayed, asking God for the strength to go on. She felt completely devoid of any hope or reason to keep going. All of a sudden a gust of wind blew through the trees behind her. The leaves started to rustle and the tree branches started to sway. A small voice told her to turn and look at them. She turned and looked, and the voice asked her, "Do you see the wind?"

"No, I do not," she answered.

"But you know it's there, right?"

"Yes, I do," Anuta answered.

"Well, you can't see me either, but I am here. So get up and go do what you need to. And if you start to doubt, just look at the trees."

Anuta found the strength to go on. She whistled for the horse and it trotted right over. Anuta, holding her baby with one arm, climbed back onto the horse and continued on her way.

When she got to the headquarters, she was given four potatoes, a small bunch of radishes and one head of cabbage and was told it should last for one week. She retorted that it would not last even one day. She left, knowing there was going to be a lot of starvation at the hands of the government, and fearing that there would soon be a lot of theft in order for people to survive.

Pulled from the Ashes: The Letter

Her friend had informed her and Misha earlier about the confiscation of the gardens, so they had stored up food in their root cellar. Before being taken to prison, Misha had sold horseshoes and frequently had hired himself out to the nomads, and had been paid with either gold or grain, so she had enough grain and potatoes. With her stepson bringing meat home every so often, they were going to be fine, but she had to keep going for rations, or it would raise suspicion.

Maxim had filed papers with his adopted country and with China for the extraction of his relatives. The United States government was willing to receive them, but China was stonewalling. When representatives of the USA took up an inquiry to the Chinese government as to why they were being stonewalled, they were told that the family was happy living where they were and did not want to leave.

When Anuta received a letter from Maxim stating what he was told, she wrote back to him. Her letter was brief and said only, "Please help us; they are lying to you. Please help us."

When Maxim received her short letter, he contacted many agencies, including the Tolstoy Foundation in New York City, which sent reporters to the village. The Chinese government knew the exact day and time that they would be in Arsalon, so the villagers were ordered to spruce up, dress well, look happy and smile a lot.

Julia was out playing with her friends in the village square and her brothers were off somewhere exploring caves with their cousin Dima when the reporters showed up; someone had driven them into the village in a wagon. Julia saw the shiny shoes, the well-pressed pants, white shirts and ties and their trench coats with strange things held by straps hanging on their necks. A bright light flashed from these strange objects when something on top of them was pressed. Julia just knew these were angels who had come to take them away and was overcome with emotion; she sat on the ground right where she had been standing, put her face in her hands and began to weep.

One of these reporters took several pictures of her. When they found out who her mother was, they interviewed Anuta, who held back nothing. She told the men about the terrible hardship that they were enduring and about her husband's imprisonment for a letter that he received from his brother. When they heard what she had to say, the reporters promised her that her family would not be forgotten like a sleeping dog; the reporters would do whatever they could to help.

25

Exodus

One typical morning Anuta baked cottage cheese pies, Julia's favorite. Suddenly a knock at the door startled everyone. Anuta opened the door ever so slightly and peeked out to see who it was. There stood an unfamiliar nomad woman and her son, both with uncombed hair, their faces dirty, and their clothes severely worn and torn. She told Anuta that her husband and the rest of her tribe had been murdered. Their sheep and camels had been driven off and their possessions taken. She and her son had survived because her husband had thrown them down into a shallow well where they stayed hidden, and they had been going from village to village begging for food ever since. Anuta gave each of them a cottage cheese pie, hot and fresh from the oven. They took them gratefully, took a few steps away from the door and devoured them.

The woman and her son stayed in the village for the rest of the morning. Julia's heart ached as she kept an eye on them. They were much sadder and poorer than anyone else in the village. The boy constantly cried for something to eat, but there was nothing with which to feed him. The villagers wanted to help, but had to be very careful with the food themselves.

Later that morning Julia, quietly playing by the river, saw the woman pull the little boy, no older than she, into the river where it was deep. Julia hid out of sight. She thought the woman was going to give her son a bath. Instead, she put both hands on his head and pushed him under the water. The boy fought as hard as he could but eventually became still. The woman pulled his dead body out of the water and onto the bank. She scooped his body into her arms and began sobbing loudly. Julia was horrified at what she had just seen but continued to stay out of sight behind a thick growth of bushes. After a long cry, the woman walked into the river, where it was deep. She deliberately went limp and disappeared under the water. When she didn't come back up, Julia ran home to tell her mother about it.

Several people went and took the little boy and buried him. They looked for the woman, but she had been washed downstream. A few days later someone stumbled on her body and she was buried beside her son.

Julia thought life should be more precious than this. Why would the woman give up hope so easily? But though she had told her mother about this tragedy, her own secrets haunted her yet. All this time, the nocturnal visits from the demon had continued. Julia's heart had begun to harden, and she didn't care anymore if he showed up or not.

One day she and her friends were playing in a little abandoned house just outside the village. A Chinese woman appeared out of nowhere, squatted down in front of Julia, took her in her arms and gave her a hug. She had soft hands. Julia had never met anyone with hands as soft as hers. The woman reached into a pocket and pulled out a carrot. Julia loved them. The woman gave the carrot to her and told her she was safe now. Julia wasn't sure what she meant but took the carrot anyway. She started to run to her friends but remembered she had forgotten to thank the woman; she spun around, but the woman was gone.

Several nights had gone by, and the demon had not returned. She wondered if this is what the Chinese woman meant by her being safe now. This was good, very good. Julia kept her eye out for that woman to thank her but never saw her again.

Anuta's friend came over again with more bad news. Tanya and her family were going to be arrested and taken to a concentration camp in two days. Again taking her loaf, she left.

Immediately Anuta went to Tanya's and reported this news to her. That night Tanya and her family grabbed only the clothes and blankets they needed along with some food and left on foot. Dima was fifteen, Feodor six, Petro three and Anya only six months old when Tanya and Sergey grabbed them and ran. They hid out in deep natural overgrown ditches three kilometers outside the village.

Anya was Tanya's crybaby. The soldiers searching for them were drawing near when Anya started crying, so Tanya placed her hand over her mouth to keep her silent. The more Anya fought, the tighter Tanya's hand became until Anya passed out. Tanya was frantic. Had she smothered her little girl? When the soldiers left, Tanya shook her, and she opened her eyes. They stayed in that ditch a few more days and then set out for Kalgatone.

Over time, families disappeared from the village. Some ran away; others were taken to concentration camps. Julia would be playing with children one day, the next their house was empty, and no one knew where they were. Terrible lawlessness broke out everywhere. People were being murdered, so at night everyone slept in their root cellars for safety.

The family of Julia's friend Irina remained, so they played together, fearing they would not see each other the next day.

Julia and Irina went to a wild blueberry patch to pick berries. They smelled something terrible but kept picking until they stumbled upon a person lying under a bush. He was dead, and the source of the terrible smell. They grabbed their berries and ran home. They were not allowed to go out again.

26

Liberation

Anuta started to feel herself giving up. Makar was her big boy; he assumed a lot of responsibilities at the age of seven. He constantly assured his mother that he would protect her and his siblings. If not for him, she probably would have given up. But he kept her hope alive in the midst of such hopelessness.

Then one day the children watched a well-dressed man ride into the village straight to their house and knock on the door. They saw their mother open the door. The man did not ask if she were the one he sought; he just handed her a letter, then turned and left without saying a word. The children ran inside to see what was happening. Their mother just held this strange letter. The envelope was stiff, not as thin as tissue like most letters, and was sent from a town about fifteen kilometers northeast. When at last she opened it, it said that she and the children needed to be in a certain place by noon the next day for passport photographs and that her husband and stepson were soon going to be released. After reading the letter several times to make sure her eyes were not deceiving her, and as if this were a lifeline for all of them, she tucked it deep into a jacket pocket so it would not be mislaid.

Fearing there might be jealous people that would harm them, she carefully instructed the children to stay in the yard.

There were almost no children to play with anymore. Julia put her sister in a little wagon and rolled her around the yard. Petro went up to the hayloft to play with the kittens. Makar took a homemade slingshot and shot annoying black crows out of a tree next to the house. Julia took interest in that and asked him if she could try. She took the slingshot, found a pebble and reversed it. Instead of aiming it at the crows, she had it aimed at herself. Just as she was about to release the pebble, Makar saw it. He placed his hand in front of her face, and the pebble made a thump as it bounced off. He then taught her the proper way to use the slingshot. They had fun the rest of the day shooing away the crows, which were migrating; the crows stopped every year at the village to fill up on grain. This year there was no grain to share so the crows had to keep moving.

When the children went in for supper, their mother told them to go to bed early as they had to walk to the place the next day since their horses had been taken from them. The walk would be long and tiring but worth it in the end. They were finally going to America to be with their Uncle Maxim whom they had not yet met.

Katiya was not even a year old, Petro not quite two and a half, Julia five and Makar seven. They knew they were going to live with someone called freedom. They wondered if she were a nice person and if she would like them.

Early the next morning, Anuta got up and climbed out of the root cellar. She made a hot breakfast and packed some bread and honey and venison jerky into a wooden box. She went to the river, filled two jugs and woke the children. She quickly dressed them, combed Julia's hair and braided it. Everyone sat down and ate a big breakfast and drank their milk from the one cow that was

212

left for the whole village. People took turns milking her and hoped she didn't die or get stolen.

As soon as there was enough daylight to see, they headed out, leaving behind Irina's family, the only Russians left in the village. Anuta carried Katiya, Makar the food box, Julia the water jugs and Petro just followed. They walked and walked. Since they had no socks, they wore old rags inside the little boots that their father had made them. Occasionally Anuta sat the three children down, unwrapped their feet and checked them for blisters. She re-wrapped them so their feet would rub in different places.

The children were tired and encouraged each other by saying "America" over and over until they finally reached their destination. It was a little shack with a sheet hanging on a wall and a camera opposite. Their pictures were taken and after a long wait they were given their passports and sent away. On the way home they found a grassy spot and sat down to eat lunch. Julia was glad that a lot of the water had been drunk. The jugs would be much lighter. Makar now had an empty box to carry, and he was glad for that too.

Two weeks went by and Makar and Julia were not allowed to venture too far from home. The communists who were still in the village started making fun of them. By this time Makar and Julia were bored because there was no one to play with them. So Makar asked his mother if he and his sister could take the chicken trough out on the river to use as a little boat. After much pleading, she allowed them to take it out to where the water was only waist deep. So Makar and Julia went to the chicken coop, scooped all the grain out of the trough and carried it out to the river. It floated when they put it in the water, so they got in and drifted downstream. Using long sticks that Makar cut from tree branches, they poled back upstream. After a long fun time, they took the trough back to the chicken coop. When they walked into the cabin, their father was sitting on the bed, holding their sister Katiya and adoring her. He was a thin, frail-looking man, not at all like they remembered him. But he was home! Now if only their brother Ivan would come home, they would once again be a whole family.

Three days later Makar and Julia were playing Hide from the Enemy and decided to try playing in a tall large round growth of stinging nettles. This would be a great place. They crawled into the center and felt its wrath. They cut out the middle growth with a knife that Makar had snitched out of the kitchen. Both were covered in welts when they came back into the house and announced that the family now had a great hiding place in the stinging nettle patch. Misha and Anuta chuckled proudly over their children.

That afternoon as they ate lunch, there was a light knock at the door. Anuta opened it, and there stood the three American reporters with a translator. She excitedly invited them in as she turned to her husband to tell him about their previous visit.

The reporters informed them both that the whole village would be allowed to leave and that reporters from England would come by in a few hours. Their story had gone throughout the whole free world. Several countries were willing to accept them. Those in concentration camps would be set free as well and all who were imprisoned were coming home; China had lost out.

Maxim made so much noise the whole world had to listen.

Hours later Ivan came walking home, accompanied by over half the people of the village. The reporters were there to take pictures and to interview every adult.

The next day a large beast came rolling into the village and frightened Julia so much that she screamed when she saw it. A man sat in a large strange wagon with four rubber wheels that moved by itself; no horses were pulling it. The beast made a rumbling sound as it moved along and pulled itself into the yard of the military post. Julia ran screaming into the cabin where her parents were packing. She was so terrified of this thing that she wet herself. Misha swept her into his arms to calm her, and after she quieted down her mother gave her a different pair of underpants. Her father took her hand and they walked out to see what frightened her.

When Misha saw the truck, he explained to his daughter that this was a wagon that did not need horses. "It is the horseless wagon that is going to take us out of this village. The reporters have hired a man to come take us away from here. We leave tomorrow."

Julia finally gathered enough courage to walk over to it and her father lifted her up so she could look inside. The driver saw her, honked the horn and waved at her. The honking sound seemed so funny; she could not stop laughing for a long time.

Anuta's friend came over again and told her that the plan was to let them go but to search everyone on the border of Red and Free China. They would be ruthless and tear out all the lining of everything. After she reported this, Anuta tearfully hugged her and thanked her for being such a good friend. They knew they were never going to see each other again. The woman took a loaf of bread and left.

Now Anuta and Misha had to figure out a way to take their gold across the border. Anuta went to the chicken coop, pulled out of the manure pile all the gold coins and jewelry that she had obtained through the years, unwrapped them, took out and put on a pair of earrings and one ring. She had several more to take over the border. Misha melted the coins down, made a bracelet loose enough that he could slide it up on Julia's forearm and put it on her wrist. A lot of gold, it would pay Maxim back for all his expenses. Since Julia was the keeper of the gold, they put all the jewelry into a leather pouch and sewed it into Julia's underpants under the thigh. They instructed her to be very careful never to take them off unless taking a bath or going to the bathroom, and she was never to pull up her sleeves but always to keep them down to conceal the bracelet.

Misha and his family and two other couples climbed on the back of the truck with their possessions. When the driver started the engine, backed out of the yard and drove out of the village, the adults let out a loud long hurrah. They were on to a new life adventure. The children sat silently. Everyone was emotionally exhausted. Petro and Katiya were rocked to sleep from the motion of the truck. One man was sitting too close to the exhaust. He threw up all over Julia, but she never complained. Her mother cleaned her off as best she could in the cramped truck.

After the first day the truck stopped and let them off in a small town. Arrangements were made for further travel. The truck left; a horse-drawn wagon would pick them up the next day. While the others went into a small building so Misha, his son and the other four people could get their passport photos taken, Anuta and the four children waited on a vacant lot.

They had nowhere to spend the night. They found a pile of hay on the ground on the same lot, so Misha covered himself and everyone else with it. They all slept so soundly that morning arrived too soon. Anuta took out bread and salt pork bellies and everyone wolfed them down. They wanted more, but the food had to be rationed to last until they caught the train that would take them across the border.

For another six days they journeyed by wagon until they reached the border. One night they slept in a large cave with a family of nomads.

Everyone was going to be searched, the two couples with them first of all. Their boots were removed, anything that was lined was ripped out, and all their clothes were spread all over the ground. Misha laid a blanket on the ground and told Julia to lie on it and act sick. She had never been sick a day in her life, but she had seen how her brother Makar acted when he had a fever, so she lay down and quietly moaned. When they were being searched, everything was torn up. They took Anuta's earrings and ring. But after one look at Julia, they did not even come close to her, not even to take off her boots. They did not want what she had.

Finally the train arrived, and everyone got on. The conductor recognized Misha; they had served in Chiang Kai-shek's army together. As the train pulled out of Red China and into Free China, he came over to Misha and declared that he and his family were now free. Misha broke into tears and wept a long while. His family were no longer in the mouth of the serpent waiting to be swallowed. They were free!

The train rolled on for four days, then came to a station in Hong Kong. Everyone was amazed at the tall buildings and paved streets. From there they got on a bus and were taken to the Kowloon Hotel, were assigned rooms and were shown where the bathrooms were. Once again they were amazed at the flushing toilets. From there they were taken to the assembly hall of the hotel for vaccinations. Anuta's temperature was high, as was Makar's. Everyone else was normal, so they were vaccinated. Anuta and Makar were to be taken to a hospital because there was a typhoid outbreak. One look at Anuta's and Makar's tongues, and they knew it was typhoid. They had been rescued from one enemy but were now contending with another.

Anuta made arrangements with one of her traveling companions to take care of Petro and Katiya.

Ivan found freedom too heady, fell in with the wrong crowd and was gone most of the time.

Misha volunteered to have Julia with him, but when his wife and son were taken to the hospital, he fell apart. Misha made friends with a man in the hotel and they both found comfort in alcohol. They stayed away all day, either in the man's room or with other people they met, and drank. Misha would leave Julia by herself two to three days at a time.

A janitor noticed that she went to the cafeteria by herself and played alone. He started sequestering and molesting her during the day with no one to come to her aid. She told a woman, only to be called a liar, because everyone thought him a very nice man, so she started to play quietly in the kitchen. The cooks knew she was all alone and didn't mind having her around.

At the end of each day, after the janitor left, she would go back to her room. One evening while on her way, she was glad to meet up with her grandmother. Julia wanted to speak up about her ordeal but was afraid that Anya would tell her sick mother, so she never said a word to her, nor to anyone else. When her grandparents, aunts and uncles, also released from the grip of communism, arrived at the hotel and learned of Anuta's illness, they went to see Anuta at the hospital only to find out that Julia was at the hotel by herself and had been for the past month. After frantically searching for her, they were overjoyed to find her safe, or so they thought.

Finally Julia had playmates, but she missed Petro and Katiya. She hadn't seen them since her mother and brother were taken away. She hardly saw her father, and when she did, he was drunk and angry. She preferred not to see him at all.

One evening they were served oranges, bananas and cheese with their meal. Never having seen oranges and bananas before, not knowing they had to be peeled, they started eating the skins

218

first. Trying not to be rude, they swallowed it. Someone noticed and came over to the table and showed them how to peel them.

Well, the cheese was tasty, and Alixey decided he would go to the market and buy some. He set out the next day, walked all around the market and found several in a bag. All the adults gathered around while Alixey pulled a pocket knife out and sliced it onto a plate. They all took a slice and started to chew as the children watched. All of a sudden they started to spit into their hands and ran to the bathroom to rinse their mouths. When they returned, they put the cheese back into a bag. When Afonase asked about what he had just seen, his grandfather told the children that they had just eaten soap. So the joke was on them; they had washed out their own mouths with soap.

Another month passed, and finally Julia's mother and brother came home. Both of their heads were almost bald; their hair had fallen out from the high fever. They were thin and pale, and they needed to rest at least two more weeks before they could travel.

Anuta's parents and her siblings Mark, Lara, and Katiya were moving to Argentina to grow tomatoes. Tanya, Feta and Natasha were moving to Brazil to grow wheat. They had no American sponsors; they had to go elsewhere. Again Anuta fell into a depression and cried a lot.

Misha's sister Anna was moving back to Russia to a town that had been named for their father. She obtained permission to go say goodbye to her brother and sister-in-law. When she arrived, she found her brother drunk and his wife in tears and scolded her brother with so much force that he stopped drinking. She understood that he had been tortured in prison. He had been put through the Chinese water torture and the hot house, and many other devices were used to break him and make him renounce America, such as one in which he had to sit under a table until someone knocked on it three times. A man would knock once and then leave for two days. He would then come back and knock one more time, then leave again for several more days before knocking a third time. And of course the food for all the prisoners was only one slice of bread per day. They were put to work in the fields. The ones who rationed the one slice into three small meals lived. Those who ate it all at once died. She knew he had been broken inside and was doing all he could to dull the memories. But he had five children who were counting on him.

She then comforted Anuta and encouraged her to be strong for Misha. Like a lost ship in a fog, he would drift to her strength.

Anuta remembered the wind in the trees and found strength in God.

So Anna took care of Petro and Katiya until her sister-in-law and nephew got well. Misha knew he would never see his sister again. They parted with promises to correspond by letter.

27
The Ship

Today they would board the Pan Am Cruise ship! Loaded with tourists of all nationalities, she would stop in Japan to unload several people, in Hawaii for a day-long tour, travel south around South America, back through the Panama Canal, and then steam to San Francisco. Misha had read about ships in school; Anuta had no idea what would be involved, but promised herself to remain calm.

A bus took them to the ship. As they got off, they could see her from a distance. As they walked closer, she grew bigger and bigger, blacker and blacker. Small round windows were set in the side. Above the deck was a rail behind which several people could be seen throwing gaily colored ribbons. Others waved from the dock. The air smelled wet and salty. Seagulls flew all around; people threw them scraps of food.

Makar, Julia, and Petro stood and looked this big black ship over. They decided she was absolutely majestic, a good ship. Everyone seemed to be filled with joy. Some people whistled, others waved.

Misha put his arm around his wife and told everyone that this ship was their salvation; she was going to carry them to a new life in America. There would be cars just like in Hong Kong. Once they got on the ship, they would not understand the language. Chinese and Russian were not spoken in America. So they were to be polite and not bother anyone.

Once on the ship, Anuta, Petro and the girls were taken to one cabin. Misha and the other boys were taken to one on the opposite side, the only two empty cabins available. Before long they were on their way. The ship swayed a little, but not like the chicken trough that Makar and Julia had taken out on the river.

Katiya developed diarrhea and Anuta got sick but did not know why. The crew noticed her suffering but could not communicate with her. After announcing over the loudspeaker that they needed a Chinese or Russian speaker to go to the doctor's office, a sweet Russian-speaking woman showed up and they went to Anuta's cabin. The doctor examined her, told her she had seasickness and gave her pills. He also told her that she was eating food she wasn't used to and passed it on to her baby through her milk, upsetting Katiya's tummy. He gave her drops to put into Katiya's mouth. The next day both were well again, with everyone relaxed and enjoying themselves.

They stood out from everyone else, being dressed in old mended clothes. The other women, in contrast, dressed in beautiful silky clothes with shiny shoes, while the men wore shorts and shirts that were not homemade. Their clothes flowed so nicely in the gentle breeze, and they wore something called sneakers.

One crew member took Makar and Julia to a dimly lit room with rows of seats and sat down in the middle row. They thought they had done something wrong and were being punished, so they sat quietly. Before long many more people came into the room, and the room was almost full. Makar and Julia wondered why they were being punished, and why the others were so happy.

Before too much longer a screen up front lit up and a long-eared rabbit and a black duck started chasing each other around on the screen. Who knew that they could talk? Makar and Julia did not understand what was said, but it was entertaining.

Julia learned two American words from the rabbit and duck: safety pin and magic. Later, from a full length feature movie, Julia learned the words yes and help, repeating them in her mind so she would not forget.

The ship docked in Japan, and people disembarked. Then, with a full brass band and saluting soldiers, the ship was sent off.

To see the dolphins trying to outrun the ship was so wonderful! The air smelled sweet and the ocean was so clear, the bottom could be seen.

The next stop was Hawaii, where Anuta and Misha got off to look around. Makar and Julia were told to stay on the ship and be good. At the end of a long day their parents returned. Many others returned and one gave Julia a lei. Well, she had to see what held it together, so she went below, took it apart and dropped the petals on the floor. The janitor scolded her. She knew by the tone of his voice.

The ship's captain heard this and gently walked up to her and took her by the hand. He led her to a room with pictures on the walls, a red carpet, a desk with a chair by it, and another on the opposite side of the room. He then sat down in front of the desk and took both of Julia's hands and in a soft voice said or asked her something. She did not understand him, so she answered him with "Safety pin. Magic. Help. Yes."

The captain chuckled and pulled open a drawer in his desk and took out a doll. It was so very beautiful! It wore a shiny colorful dress and had long shiny black hair, blue eyes, and red lips. He gave it to Julia. She took it and laughed with delight. He stood up, went to the door and opened it. Julia left running to find her mama and show it off.

The Panama Canal was long and boring. Two other ships were ahead of them. The deck was crowded with people watching this event. When it was their turn, something like a gate pulled off to the side; the ship sailed in, and the gate closed. There was another gate in front of them. Water filled the canal as the ship gently rocked back and forth. After a while, the gate in front slid open, and the ship sailed through. On she sailed for a few days. The children were tired of the water and wanted to move on to something different, even though the food was so delicious and there was lots of it.

When the ship docked in San Francisco, they collected their measly luggage and walked to a train station. Misha followed directions that were written out on a long piece of paper. They had to wait until the next morning before a train would take them to New York City, where Maxim would pick them up. The railroad employees noticed they were foreigners and brought them food and beverages.

After getting on the train and being taken to their seats, they were on their way. Anuta had some dried bread cubes, which she rationed out to everyone. It had to last until New York. They were grateful to have it, and no one complained. Everyone sat quietly and looked out the windows, getting out of their seats only to go to the bathroom, while the train clacked over the tracks as it rolled along. Some people tried to talk to them, but quickly discovered they were foreigners.

28

New York

As the train pulled into the station Misha saw his brother Maxim and Alexander, taller than he remembered, standing and waiting. Misha patiently guided his family off the train, and as they all stepped off, Misha and Maxim grabbed each other like giddy school girls. Alexander quickly joined them. After a proper greeting, Maxim walked over to Julia, swept her up into his arms and hugged her. He turned to Misha and remarked how she looked so much like him and their sister.

Everyone kept looking around at the tall buildings, the black smooth streets for the cars, the sidewalk for the people. They felt they had just arrived in heaven, it was so clean and orderly. All the people seemed so kind, and they really did smile just as Maxim had written in his letter.

Misha, Anuta and Katiya got into Maxim's car, Makar, Julia and Petro into Alexander's. After about an hour, they arrived at Maxim's home in Congers. It was a fortress. No chickens or geese around and no smell of manure spoiled the scene: the driveway light pale and smooth, even a garage for the car. The lawn was green and even, just like a carpet. Walking into the house, they were equally amazed: white walls, hung with pretty pictures;

beautiful furniture placed all around, and the carpet just as pretty as the lawn.

Maxim had three beautiful girls, shy and quiet at first. Mary was a little younger than Julia. Jane and Nancy were about Petro's and Katiya's ages.

Misha was interested in what made the cars run. Maxim led him out to the garage, poured a few drops of gasoline on the cement floor, took a match and lit it.

They did not notice Julia watching curiously from around the corner. When they went outside, Julia, still standing there, saw a little water puddled on the cement floor. She went to her cousin Mary and enlisted her help, but each time they dropped a lit match into the puddle, it went out.

Maxim and Misha walked back into the garage and saw what they were doing. Maxim felt he needed to discipline Mary for playing with the matches, but Julia owned up to instigating all of it. So her uncle gave her a choice between a spanking or time in the corner. She asked him if the spanking would hurt.

Maxim answered her with a question: "What good is a spanking if it does not hurt?"

Would she have to stand in the corner a long time?

He nodded his head and said, "Yes, a long time."

Julia thought about it and chose the corner.

So Maxim pointed, and she went without protest. Her cousin Mary went out back, brought in a lawn chair and sat down to keep her cousin company.

When her time was served, She was brought into the front room where she saw a man in a box making an announcement. Julia was amazed that a man could fit into a box and queried her uncle about it. He told her, "Oh, it's just some guy we caught and put in there."

Julia was outraged. "You said people are free here, yet you have a man in a box!"

Maxim laughed at her innocence and tried to explain. Julia was not satisfied until he changed the channel and she saw different images.

After three weeks at Maxim's house, his wife told him that they were too crowded and that his family had to leave. Anuta's second cousin Kuzma was one of the twenty who made it over the Himalayas into India and then to America with Maxim. He and his wife Rada and their two boys lived in a small two bedroom apartment. After they got permission from their landlord, they took them in. Misha immediately went to work as a carpenter for Maxim's boss.

A month later they cut the gold bracelet off Julia's wrist and sold it along with the jewelry. After paying Maxim back, enough money remained for a down payment on a house.

Anuta did not like city life. She missed having cows and chickens, a garden and wild berries. Misha and Kuzma found the perfect one-hundred acre ranch in Youngsville: the ranch house, an older duplex but ideal for their situation, had three bedrooms on one side for Kuzma and Rada and two stories including four bedrooms and a basement for Misha and his family; a spacious two story barn; two roomy buildings to house chickens, one for Rada, one for Anuta; a building they could modify as a bath house; ample area to fence off for a pig pen; and a sizeable smoke house made for everything they could want: running water and electricity, but no water heater, two ponds, one with fish and a well next to where the bath house would be, lots of wild blackberries and boysenberries, wild blueberries, strawberries and raspberries; wild purple plum trees and a couple of peach trees, and five acres of apple trees! All of it fenced in for the cattle, although the barbed wire needed replacing. The different pastures were separated with rock walls.

A down payment was made on this property, and the rest was financed. Misha and Anuta were nervous about the payments and even more nervous about the bank owning it until it was paid off. Once they moved in, Misha and Anuta gathered the children and explained to them that everyone had to conserve so the property could be paid off sooner. They were told not to be wasteful with toilet paper, electricity or food.

The barbed wire was replaced one weekend and cows acquired. The pigpen was fenced and pigs brought in. Next came chickens. Anuta did not want geese or ducks, as she was told that she would have to buy special food for them because the soil lacked necessary minerals, but the chickens prospered and were often mistaken for turkeys. They planted an extensive vegetable garden and a separate potato patch that took up an acre.

Misha dug a root cellar next to the house for storing the harvest. Having milk, eggs, meat, and an abundance of vegetables and hay from the pastures, they were very nearly self-sufficient.

Anuta, once again prosperous and happy, was blissfully unaware of her husband's renewed chanting in the basement. He invited demons into the house: fear, anger, division and many others. Julia and Petro saw them frequently, but were not allowed to speak of it. Before long their family life—constant bickering and angry outbursts—was reminiscent of the demons that inhabited their home. Everyone felt terrified all the time. Furniture moved around on its own. Strange breezes blew inside the house, and during the night footsteps and other noises were heard.

Julia started questioning her mother about God but was not comforted by her answers. Anuta told her that they lived under

God's law of sin and death. If you sinned, you died, after which
angels took you through a review of your life; these carried a
scale, and as each situation was judged it was placed on either the
positive or negative side. If in the end the positive outweighed
the negative, then you went to heaven, otherwise you were
handed off to the demons who followed you during this time of
judgment. They grabbed your soul, dragged you down to hell
and tortured you for eternity. Anuta also told Julia that one of a
thousand men were saved but only one of a hundred thousand
women, because they were cursed for Eve's sin of eating the
forbidden fruit.

Julia became depressed, thinking that she had no life on earth
and probably would go to hell in the end. Her father had begun
abusing her. He was kind to her siblings, especially to Petro and
Katiya, his favorites, who got to sit on his lap. Julia, on the other
hand, he often threatened to kill. Since they lived in Youngsville
and Misha worked in Nyack, eighty miles away, he left early
Monday mornings and returned on Friday evenings, giving her
peace during the week. On the weekends she avoided him to the
best of her ability except at mealtime. She ate quietly and avoided
eye contact with him as much as possible. If she irritated him, he
would either grab her by the hair and drag her to a corner or
threaten her.

Her mother saw all of this but could not help. Misha would
often beat her if she took Julia's side. He bragged about his power
as a warlock and boasted to Anuta that he had a spell that would
turn her into a comatose vegetable. He petrified her, and she
dared not ask for help nor even tell anyone.

Julia hardened her heart in order to cope. She feared her
earthly father and her Creator, who was so mean to make her go
through such dreadful judgment after a terrible life.

Misha worked and handed his money over to Anuta, the penny pincher, and in three years they had enough to pay off the property. After they got the deed, Anuta asked her husband to sponsor her sister Tanya and her family to America. He agreed and two years later, they had enough to pay their way, with a job waiting for Sergey.

Three months later, when Tanya and her family flew into New York City, Misha was there waiting for them. Both families lived happily together for another three months. Sergey, too, left for work on Monday mornings and returned on Friday nights. Because of the company Misha hid his anger toward his daughter. She thought he had finally learned to love her. But when their guests saved enough money to buy a car and to rent an apartment, they moved to Piermont to be closer to Sergey's job.

The abuse and demonic activity resumed. Now Julia was constantly invited to serve Satan or die. She told the demon she preferred death rather than to serve that loser. The demons began attacking her physically, when she slept and at times during the day. She never knew when or where. She found solitude at school, where they never bothered her.

One day at her mother's request she had gone out to pick wild berries for jam when she heard—coming toward her!—a very eerie sound. She was not going to give the demons the pleasure of a reaction, so she kept picking. Suddenly, passing in front of her, it seemed as the air was becoming plastic and folding up on itself in new dimensions. She had never seen such a thing before. It paralyzed her with terror, but she kept a poker face and continued to pick the berries. Her mother paraded naked in front of her, but she knew it was not her mother; a mother had a scent that only a child would recognize and be comforted by. This thing parading in front of her was neither. All of a sudden she heard a voice, the same one that had spoken to her when the snake was chasing her, say, "Get home now! These things mean to harm you."

Julia picked up her berry basket and headed home. Her mother was kneading bread dough. Julia walked up, leaned into her and took a sniff. This was her mama, the sweet loving woman who suffered along with her. But neither one had a way out. Julia never said one word to her. Mama had enough to contend with already.

One year later, Tanya and Anuta and their spouses sponsored Georgiy and Feta, who moved in with Anuta and Misha. Once again the abuse and demonic activity stopped. Feta had three daughters, and everyone played well together on the ninety-three acres of pasture and seven of woods. Georgiy was hired by the same construction company where Misha and Sergey worked. Once again it had become a happy home. Once again Julia thought her father had learned to love her. She wanted so much to be loved by him. But in the spring, Feta and Georgiy, too, rented an inexpensive apartment in Piermont.

Summers Anuta would send Julia to live with her aunts and cousins in Piermont to get some rest and rejuvenation. Before long more and more Russians arrived in the United States; now they were choosing to move to Woodburn, Oregon in the Willamette Valley. Being farmers, they had heard of the fertile soil of the valley.

Ivan wanted to check it out for himself. He flew into Portland, rented a car and drove to Woodburn. There he met up with some of his childhood friends and fellow prisoners from the concentration camp. Between the people he knew and the money they were making, he fell in love with the area.

When he returned home and showed his family his pictures, Misha and Anuta started considering the move. Tanya and Feta, along with their husbands, also decided to go the following spring.

Ivan fell in love and was soon married, in a three day celebration. One year later Shura gave him a daughter. They needed a home, so Kuzma and Rada sold their portion of the property to Ivan and Shura, and they moved to a little farm nearby in White Rock.

Anuta missed her sisters, who now lived in Oregon, and she wanted her children to attend a church of her own religion, lest they drift away from it. Misha's heart was softened, so they took a trip to visit Tanya and Feta, who received them warmly and led them on a tour of Silver Creek Falls and of a hot springs only seventy miles away. Misha met up with some of his prison-mates, with people with whom he grew up and with military buddies. When they got home, they put their ranch on the market.

The children were excited to be reunited with their cousins, yet sad to part with their friends and neighbors, one family in particular, a black family whom the children loved. The father was a police detective in New York City, and his wife a nurse in the city hospital, so they were home only on weekends. His mother took care of their children and niece who lived with them. She was Makar and Julia's friend, and they loved her very much. The man never learned what went on in Julia's family, as she never told anyone, but she listened to his advice. He did not know she had adopted him as a surrogate father. When they sold the ranch and moved away, Julia grieved as if for a death in the family. As a minor she could not just pick up the phone and call. She wrote occasionally, but finally she lost touch.

Misha was now with his old buddies and started drinking again, which brought the meanness out in him; the abuse intensified, and the death threats grew worse. One day he came at Julia with a large chunk of firewood. As he raised it over his head, he told Julia to repent for all her sins, because he was going to kill her. He had no use for her and couldn't stand to be around her. Julia stood still and welcomed it. Her heart had been broken so deeply that only the grave could protect her from him. She closed her eyes and waited as Misha lowered the deadly instrument.

Anuta came just in time to see this and threw herself at him. He lost his balance and fell. "Run, Julia!" she called out.

Julia took off running. She ran out of the house, onto the road and into town. From there she called a friend from a pay phone; he came and got her. Evenings Julia had been working as a translator in a clinic and so had some money on her, to which her friend added. He took her to a motel not too far away, where she rented a room for four nights. Being careful with her money, she bought a loaf of bread and some lunch meat. She had to make herself eat; her stomach was so upset by the ordeal that she lost her appetite. Fearing her father would find her and finish what he started, she did not call home.

The motel owner saw her picture on the television and notified the police, who came and got her and were as nasty to her as if she had robbed a bank or killed someone. After scolding her, they planned to take her back to her parents, but when Julia broke down and asked them to shoot her, telling them of the years of abuse and bruises she had had to hide, and of those on her heart that would never heal, they first accused her of lying. She stuck to her story, however, and they came to believe her and took her to a shelter until they could investigate and talk to the rest of the family.

After the investigation was completed, the police told Julia's mother that Julia would not be allowed to return home as long as her father lived there.

Misha turned his abuse toward Anuta. He poured battery acid on her while she slept. Once he came after her with a hammer, another time with an ice pick.

Meanwhile someone befriended Julia and took her to church. The minister talked about how God so loved the world that He sent His only son to die for it. Julia had never before heard of God's love. She thought He sided with her father. So she bowed her head and tearfully asked God to steal her family from the grip of Satan and to restore it.

Julia was so worried about her mother. She knew that her father would never hurt Petro and Katiya, and that Makar could take care of himself.

When Anuta had had enough and at Makar's pleading, she went to court to get a restraining order and Misha was ordered to leave the house. Again she went to court and got Julia back.

Julia tried to be happy but was too broken to carry on. She felt no sadness, no joy, no hope. Her identity had drained from her; some said she no longer had a personality. No matter what she did, she felt worthless and useless. Her mother encouraged her to go to church, but when she went to her mother's church, she felt even worse. All they talked about was the law of sin and death.

Anuta was left with the bills and four children. She had been a housewife, did not drive or own a car, had no working skills and did not speak English. She filed for divorce and was awarded child support payments, the house and property, but as they left the courthouse, Misha informed her that she would never get a penny from him. He packed up and went back to New York to his old job.

29

Sifting

There Misha met and married a woman who had a strong personality. He hit her once and was out on the street, divorced again. He met another woman twenty years his senior; neither did she put up with his rage; he had to calm down. Divorced twice already, he decided that he did not want to do it a third time, so he started to behave. He did not call or write his children, so they forgot him.

Except Julia—she did not forget. For some strange reason, she felt pity for him, and ached for his soul.

Weary of her mother's church, she quit going. Anuta believed that obedience to the law of sin and death was the only way that Julia had a small chance of salvation, but Julia did not agree. She never forgot the time when she went to church with her friend and the minister talked about God's love for everyone. But since she lived at home and was still considered a minor, she became neutral. She found a Bible and read the book of Genesis and liked it, then Exodus. Deuteronomy, however, reminded her so much of the law of sin and death that she closed the Bible and put it away.

Anuta worked as a field hand to earn enough money to replace the well. Makar and Julia dropped out of school and went to work to help her. Makar kept half the money he earned, but Julia gave all of her money to her mother. When the well and pump were paid off, Julia bought a car and rented an apartment. But she always made sure that Mama got to where she needed to go.

To avoid the constant discussion of religion, Julia fell into a group that liked to party. Although she drank very little alcohol and never took drugs, she loved the fishing trips and became quite good at it. All the fish that she and her friends caught went to her mother.

During one particular weekly trip to the grocery store, her mother asked her to walk some distance away because she was ashamed of her. Julia's friends, when they heard this, advised her to stop helping Anuta, but she loved her too much and continued to help, although verbally rejected. She could not forget all that Mama had been through and all that she had done for her. In Julia's mind, this was a way of serving God—though some of her friends told her there was no God, He was just something fearful people conjured up. Demons, however, Julia had seen with her own eyes. How did they come to be? She knew beyond a doubt that God was real. However, He seemed harsh and, because she had given up hope that He loved her, with each passing month her heart grew colder.

Julia became expert at swearing and using the name of Jesus in vain. In fact, she could curse better than anyone she knew. Once she even made a truck driver blush with her foul language. She was a very angry, hurt person, though she did not realize it at that time.

But Julia was unaware that God had put her on the heart of an elderly woman, who had been praying daily for her. One day, God opened Julia's eyes, and she began to see either a darkness or a bright light radiating out of people. No one was neutral; everyone was either bright or dark. Those surrounded by darkness also had a slimy slug-like substance all over their bodies. She thought that she must have a brain tumor or was going to have a stroke. Frightened, she went to the doctor. After a thorough checkup, he pronounced her well.

She decided to question the first person who was lit up. The next day while Julia was in the produce section, a glowing woman walked up to the apples. Julia quickly went over and asked her in her colorful language, "Why is there a light coming from you?"

The woman was not all fazed by her question. She just smiled and answered, "Well, Jesus lives in my heart. He is the one shining through me."

Julia had never heard of such a thing. The woman spoke of Jesus as if she were speaking of a friend. Julia had heard of Jesus, something about a cross, and that He had died for the people of the Old Testament. She did not even know what an Old Testament was.

She asked the woman in a forceful voice, "Well, how did He get in there? Isn't He a full-grown man? And how is your heart taking all of this?"

The woman smiled and answered ever so kindly and sweetly. Julia felt good as she spoke. There was truth in her voice. She questioned Julia about where she lived and worked. The next workday the woman brought a Bible to Julia's job, with a note telling her where to start reading.

The more Julia read, the more her lifestyle disgusted her. One day she decided to talk to Jesus. She tried to say His name, but something prevented her. She could not speak it out. The harder she tried, the more paralyzed her tongue became. She knew that the name she was trying to speak had great power and something did not want her to say it. All of a sudden her tongue was loosed. The name of Jesus rolled off her tongue, and it tasted sweet.

Julia was shaking. It had taken all her strength to accomplish this. Realizing her life was a mess, she asked this wonderful Jesus to fix it. All of a sudden there He stood before her with His arms open wide as if inviting her to come to Him. She felt terribly unclean, full of shame and guilt. When He disappeared, she crumpled to the floor and wept. She wanted Him to stay and to love her, yet she felt too dirty to be in the same room with Him.

That night she went to sleep wondering if she could get near to this Jesus. All she knew was sin and death.

God knew all that was going on in Julia's heart. She did not know it, but He had a plan to sift her, to remove all her darkness bit by bit. Later that week Julia ran into a woman who could talk about nothing but Jesus and how He saved her soul by dying on the cross for her sins. Julia kept waiting to be invited to church. Finally she asked her, "Where do you go to church? And will you take me with you?"

The woman was surprised, but the following Sunday they went together to People's Church in Salem. Julia acted just as she had done when she first arrived in New York City: she looked around in amazement. There was a wonderful peace in that place.

First the choir sang, then the congregation. The minister got up on the stage and talked about what a friend Jesus is to everyone. Julia saw the words on a wall above his head: "Jesus is the same yesterday, today, and forever."

When the minister asked for people to come up front if they wanted to receive Jesus into their hearts as their savior, Julia was there first. A man came over to her. Julia told him, "I think my heart is too hard. Jesus might not be able to get into it."

The man lovingly hugged her and whispered in her ear, "Nothing can keep Him out." He instructed Julia to repeat this prayer after him: "Jesus, I have been deeply hurt and almost destroyed by the enemy that rules my father. I ask You, please, take me just as I am. I confess that You suffered and died for me. When you were carrying my cross on your back, You were weak and thought of quitting. Then You saw me and how desperate I was. You found strength to go to the hill and died a terrible death on a cruel cross. Please, Jesus, forgive all my sins and set me free from the bondage of sin and death. Make me into an instrument for you."

Julia's face was wet with tears. As they dripped onto her blouse, she wondered how a complete stranger could know about her father and the problem that she was having with the law of sin and death. So she asked, and he told her that the Holy Spirit had revealed it to him.

She had heard of the Holy Spirit, but did not know where He fit in people's lives. The mere words "Holy Spirit" uplifted her spirit. She was told that she was now saved and would go straight to heaven when she died, and about God's grace, and what Romans 6:14 says: "For sin shall not be your master, because you are not under law, but under grace."

Julia did not know what he meant. What was grace? How could she be saved by just saying a prayer? She was feeling much freer since she had prayed. What had happened? She had to know what that prayer had done. Why was she now feeling this way?

The man understood that Julia knew nothing about the written Word, so he explained to her that Adam and Eve were placed in a beautiful garden with the best of everything. They lived together with all the animals, even tigers, lions, and bears. Every living thing ate vegetation. They were friends with God. In the garden were two trees, the tree of life and the tree of the knowledge of good and evil. Adam and Eve could eat every fruit in the garden except the fruit of the tree of knowledge. If they did, they would die. Satan tricked Eve into eating from this tree. When she did and nothing happened, she gave some to Adam and he ate. At that moment, they brought a sin nature on all mankind.

They were naked and ashamed. When God found them, He cursed the ground, the animals, and them. Now they knew fear and death. The animals suddenly had the need to kill and eat each other. God and man were no longer friends but enemies. To prevent them from eating of the tree of life and living forever with their sin nature, He drove them out of the garden. Satan now ruled the earth. And for generations, an atonement had to be made for every sin. Animals must be killed and their blood poured out.

But when the time was right, God sent His son to die an agonizing death on a cross. He corrected Adam's wrongs. It was a gift for us. Jesus bought us from Satan with His own life. All we needed to do is confess that Jesus took our sins on Himself and died with them. Through the power of the Holy Spirit, He rose again. Sin and death were conquered. Our bodies will eventually die, but our spirits will live forever in a home that is being prepared for us.

Julia now understood and could not wait to tell her family. She went straight to her mother's house, told her about the prayer and about grace. Her mother broke into tears and wept bitterly. She told Julia that Satan had clouded her mind with fairy tales. Salvation was not free; it had to be earned.

When Julia told her brother Makar about salvation, he laughed in her face; so did Petro and her sister Katiya. Her aunts, uncles and cousins all reacted the same as her mother. She was no longer invited to family functions.

Her friends scoffed and begged her to quit believing such lies when she told them about Jesus and His sacrifice for them. They told her salvation was only for the old and to have fun while she could.

Her co-workers just stared at her.

Now Julia was all alone, having distanced herself from everyone for Jesus' sake. He was not ashamed of her, and she would not be ashamed of Him.

Leaving their mother behind, Makar, Petro and Katiya grew and went on with their lives.

One Tuesday Anuta received a letter from her mother. The news was very sad: her father had come home from work but while washing up for dinner, fell over and died.

Anuta was sobbing so hard that Julia could not understand her. She went over to her mother's house immediately to comfort her. Mama was so sad! She could not live alone any more. With her mother constantly trying to re-convert her, living there would be difficult, but with God's help and grace, it would be all right.

Her mother, though over the shock, was constantly sad, even after Julia settled in, so Julia cleaned the briers out of the chicken coop and bought her chickens. When, shortly afterwards, one started brooding and hatched out five chicks, they went together to a hatchery, bought another thirty-five and slipped them under the hen during the night. The next morning the proud mother hen brought the chicks out to show them off. Hen and chicks were allowed to roam free, and Anuta livened up again watching the silly creatures walk around and scratch the earth for little grubs.

Some months later Natasha and her family moved up from South America, and six months after that, Julia's grandmother Anya, her Aunts Natasha and Katiya and Uncle Mark and their families moved to Woodburn.

Julia started attending Bible studies. Her mother occasionally brought up the subject of returning to her church, but Julia always respectfully declined. Though she continued, without much hope, to pray for her family, there seemed to be no fruit to her prayer. She knew God was listening, but as far as she was concerned, He was not moving. Mama was unchanged, and her brother Petro and sister Katiya had fallen into a bad crowd and were endangering their lives.

30

Pulled from the Ashes

As usual, Julia picked up the Bible to read. It opened to Psalm 113, and her eyes focused on verse 7. "He raises the poor from the dust and lifts the needy from the ash heap. He seats them with princes and princesses of their people." Julia read it but did not make the connection. Each time she picked up the Bible or set it down, it would open to that chapter, and her eyes would always focus on that verse. After about ten times, she got it: God was going to pull her and her family out of the ashes. Now she had hope, and told her family about it.

What she kept secret was that demons were still attacking her regularly. Sometimes her bed would dance across the room while she was in it. Other times she would be tossed out of it or grabbed from behind as she walked. Often she would be pushed while walking down the stairs.

One night at her Bible study, she could hold back the pain no longer. She burst into tears and cried for the whole two hours while the teacher taught. Afterward he came up to her to find out if she was all right. She confessed everything: the sexual and physical abuse and the demonic attacks. Quickly surrounded by caring people who prayed for her protection, she was counseled to forgive all those who hurt her. She tried, but the pain remained.

What did change was that she started seeing angels all around. Sometimes while driving, she would see a group of them, some huge, others as little as five feet tall. Some had wings, others did not. They would wave to her as she drove by.

One night when she felt at her lowest and as if no one loved her—*I've always wanted my father's love, and saw my siblings receive it, why not me?*—she tearfully told God about all her pain. Just as she had always been good at keeping things to herself and never had told her parents anything, neither did she know how to tell God anything. Her parents had not protected her, so she did not have that security ingrained in her. In her mind it was she against the world and everything against her. She fell on her bed as she told God that all she had ever wanted was to be loved. Instead, even her siblings mocked her and her own mother frequently told her that she was ashamed of her. As Julia poured her heart out, an angel scooped her into his arms and held her while she cried. This seemed to set her somewhat free.

As time went on, she struggled to be free of the demonic oppression, that invisible force that was holding her back and that threw heavy objects at her. Somehow these objects never reached her but only got so far and fell to the ground.

Then she met a young man named Randy Conger, with whom she could freely speak of her deep and even fanatical love for God. Julia shared about the demonic attacks and Randy advised her to tell her pastor; perhaps he could help. She did so the very next Sunday, but the pastor quickly referred her to another church. That pastor, too, passed her off to someone else. After several more referrals Julia came to the conclusion that these pastors were afraid of the demons and did not want to deal with her.

For thirteen more years she suffered in silence. She met Gary; they fell in love and were married. He was so kind and gentle to her, but although he knew about her suffering, he did not know how to help.

Petro moved back to New York to be near his father, who, having been diagnosed with Parkinson's, was now in a wheelchair. Julia, concerned for her brother's salvation, frequently wrote him letters about her wonderful Savior. Petro would read them, write something nasty at the bottom and mail them back. Not discouraged, she kept writing but always received hostile replies. Eventually Petro became an alcoholic and lost his job. As his stepmother was then too old to care for his father's failing health, Petro brought him back to Woodburn and left him with Ivan.

Julia had been tearfully praying for her father as well but did not have a close enough relationship with him to call and talk about his salvation. God told her to go, so with Gary's blessing, she went to Ivan's home. There sat her father, pitifully thin, incapable of even lifting a fork. One look at him and her heart melted. She asked him if he had been fed, and he showed her a dried-out cob of corn he had been given that morning.

Seeing how weak he appeared, she went home and got her husband, and together they loaded him into the car and took him to a hospital. After examining him the doctors told Julia that he had advanced Parkinson's and would need to be placed in a nursing home. They would keep him overnight for observation, but that the next day she must pick him up.

During the night she prayed to God for help, asking God to prove Himself to her father. The next morning she went to work and during her breaks called nursing homes; she found one close to home. That evening she and her husband left for the hospital to pick him up and give him the news.

Well, he had a surprise for her. During the night he had had to go to the bathroom. He had reached for the call button to get a nurse when a voice ordered him to get up and walk to the bathroom; he did so without a second thought. After he got back to his bed, it dawned on him that he was not shaking any more, and that he had walked. He held his hands out in front of him and they were steady. He could not wait to share the news with Julia.

Julia walked into her father's hospital room, with a knot in her stomach, and started to explain to him what had to happen.

He stood up and walked across the room and back to his bed. Julia's mouth dropped open as she looked at him. His hands were not shaking, nor any other part of him. Misha told her about the voice commanding him to walk to the bathroom. Julia could barely contain her joy. Her father had been healed. He did not deserve it, considering all that he had done to her and to her mother. But nobody did. It was just like God and His grace.

Julia told her father that he had been healed by her God, and he could not deny it.

That evening he walked out of the hospital, to her car, and into Julia's house. While he was there, God gave her boldness and she confronted him about the witchcraft. When she told him that God loved him so much He sent His son Jesus to die for him, her father broke into tears and repented to her and to God, renounced Satan and all the dark and terrible things that he had done and joyfully received salvation. After a month of being home alone while Julia and Gary worked, he became lonely and rented a room in a boarding house, where he thrived.

He and Anuta became friends once again. He would go over during the day, help her with her garden and do odd jobs around the house. He got in touch with his wife in New York, but she felt he would be better off near his children. When she died a few months later, Misha waited a year, and then asked Anuta to marry him again, but she turned him down. She was finally happy with her sons Makar and Ivan living on either side of her, her grandchildren at her house during the day, and Julia there every weekend to take her shopping, or anywhere else she needed to go. Two years later Misha died in his sleep with a peaceful, happy look on his face.

Shortly after this her brother Petro was diagnosed with advanced stages of hepatitis C brought on by alcoholism. The only chance of saving his life was a liver transplant. He went over to Julia's house and tearfully broke the news. When she started talking about Jesus, he left.

To get on the list for a transplant, various tests, some quite harsh, had to be performed over a three-day period to make sure he would survive the eighteen-hour surgery. After the last test he was required to spend the night for observation. He passed and was placed on a waiting list.

Petro wanted neither the surgery nor the medication that he would have to take for the rest of his life to suppress his immune system, so as he lay in bed, he reviewed his life. He had hurt others and told terrible lies. He thought of the letters and cards he had received from his sister. Thinking of the peace that the prayer she had written would bring him, he prayed with all his heart, asking God to take him home, but not while it was dark, not during the night. He rang for the nurse, gave her Julia's address and phone number, and asked her to call and thank Julia for her persistent preaching. He had prayed the prayer and now knew the healing that went along with it. He also told the nurse that after the sun came up, God would take him home. Though assured he was not going anywhere but back home, he told her he would call her into his room to witness it when it was time, and to tell his sister.

According to the nurse, he went to the window several times during the night, waiting for daylight. When the sun came up, he called her into the room and told her how much he appreciated all she had done for him. He lay down on the bed, pulled his covers up to his chin, closed his eyes and died. The nurse announced code blue over the loudspeaker. Nurses and doctors ran into the room and revived him. He opened his eyes and told them not to do that again. He closed his eyes and died again.

When Julia was notified of her brother's decision and death, she, her mother and sister went to view his body. He looked as if he were having a happy dream. His cheeks were rosy, his complexion flawless.

Even through Anuta's tears, she was amazed at his appearance and could not believe how happy he looked. After the funeral, however, she gave up. No more life in her. Six children buried. So many tears. A few months later she was diagnosed with inoperable stage-four ovarian cancer and was given one month to live.

Julia started screaming, "What about her soul, God? I can part with her in this life because You will carry me through. But I cannot part with her in eternal life. Please, God, please save her soul." She fell silent. How much more was her mother to suffer? Her mother had told her, every time they went anywhere, all about her childhood, the children she buried, and the first husband she loved. Sad and full of suffering, the stories nonetheless drew Julia close to her mother. She would miss all those wonderful stories. She loved her mother more every time she heard them.

God spoke in an audible voice and said, "I will restore her soul. Just rest in me, and I will carry you through this."

Julia watched closely for signs of salvation in her mother but saw none. One day after her mother was bedridden, Julia asked her, "Mama, are you by any chance mad at God?"

Her mother answered curtly. "Mad at God? He is God; He has seen us through so much. How could anyone be mad at God? What would we have if we did not have God?"

Well, that answered Julia's question. Her mother knew her place in God. She had another question, however. "Mama, who is Jesus to you?"

Her mother looked at Julia as if she were shocked that she called him Jesus. She answered, "You cannot just call Him Jesus. You have to call Him Jesus Christ. Besides, you have to reach a certain level of holiness to be able to speak His name."

Julia could feel her heart break, but had to press on. "Mama, don't you know that Jesus and mankind have been friends since He rose from the dead?"

Her mother seemed so saddened by what Julia was saying. She said something that crushed her. "Please, don't talk to me about your faith. You are going to go to hell for your beliefs and you are trying to talk me into going there too."

Julia decided to tell her mother everything, afraid that if she didn't she would have to carry them all alone the rest of her life. She told her about the man that came into the house and raped her when she was left alone. About being punished for wetting the bed. About being molested at the Kowloon Hotel. "Mama, Jesus is the One helping me get through my days. He is my friend and always will be."

God told Julia right at that moment to watch and see what He was going to do. She saw two angels enter the room, and it was clear that her mother did, too, by the way she would look at one, then the other. God told her to remain quiet and let the angels talk.

Pulled from the Ashes

The first angel told Anuta that Julia had been telling her the truth. The other told her that living under the law of sin and death brought only death. They took turns telling her about God's grace and what it meant, and that when she confessed her sins to another man, her sins remained. Man has a sin nature; he has no authority to forgive sin. Only Jesus could, since He took them to the cross. He had no sin nature; He was the seed of the spirit, not of man.

Anuta received everything that the angels told her, and they left. God told Julia that He was giving her mother three days to repent, and then He would take her, so she gave her mother the privacy she needed. For three days Anuta tearfully repented to Jesus for all her sins, then slipped into a coma and developed a rattle in her chest.

Anya quietly wept in a corner of the room as she watched her daughter's wrinkles disappear.

Julia walked in and let the tears fall freely. She'd been strong for Mama; now it was time to say her goodbyes. She gently pulled off the blanket, kissed her feet and thanked her for carrying her around when she was a baby. Pulling the blanket back up, she kissed each of her hands and thanked her for all the hard work they had done for her. Moving up to her forehead, she thanked her for worrying about her; to her chest for loving her; to her lips to say goodbye.

Anuta started to glow. The light radiating from her would have lit up a dark room. Her now beautiful face smiled, as if seeing something worth smiling about. She exhaled a long slow breath. There were no more.

Julia's eyes were opened and she recognized the angels as they came, lifted her mama's lovely soul from her body, floated with it up through the ceiling and then were gone.

Pulled from the Ashes

The family were amazed as they gathered around her body at how beautiful she looked, too beautiful to bury. Julia took the opportunity to explain to them that this was the way someone looked when they were forgiven for their sin. Julia told them that she was literally pulled from the ashes as it says in Psalms 113:7.

Julia was the only one of the children to go to her funeral. Makar and Katiya did not come. It broke Julia's heart, but she did not judge them for it.

A week after the funeral, Julia heard the laughter of young children. Puzzled, since no children lived nearby, she went to the window to see who had come over. No one was outside, so Julia went back to her housework. But the children's laughter continued. Then, as if something like a movie screen had dropped down in front of her, she saw five small children and one much older child, running and playing, trying to follow a woman, who looked very confident and happy. Julia did not recognize the woman or the children, but she knew that God was showing all this to her. She asked, "God, who is that woman and who are those children?"

God answered, "That is your mother and those are your brothers and sisters. She has been reunited with them as she has so desired."

Julia watched as the children played and her mother walked in a grassy meadow with gentle hills. No one wore shoes, nor had a care or worry. Slowly the screen faded and disappeared. Julia sat down and cried. Mama was finally reunited with her children, and nothing could ever hurt her again.

Months went by. Julia tried to build a relationship with her brothers and sisters, but they did not want her around because she was, as they put it, a Jesus fanatic. She pined for her mother.

The demonic attacks continued. One night as she slept, she felt a terrifying presence in the room that made her body feel weak. She opened her eyes, and Satan stood at her bedside. She was surprised at how small he was. He ordered Julia to serve him. Suddenly, Jesus appeared and told her not to answer. Satan growled and reminded Jesus that she had been dedicated to him as an infant. Jesus did not say a word, but just held out his hands, his scars clearly visible. A glowing gate dropped down between Julia and Satan and he vanished. Jesus told Julia that Satan would not be bothering her again, and then He disappeared.

Julia began having terrible fear attacks. She thought that she was going to lose her mind. Gary worried about her, and she became angry and withdrawn. This went on for months until one day, they were invited to Solomon's Porch in Hubbard, the small church where Randy Conger was pastor. Good things were happening there. Out of desperation, they went. Randy had become a great man of God and the presence of the Lord was strong in that place. Even greater attacks of fear came at Julia. Voices told her that they would kill her if she went back there again.

Ignoring them, she went back. Randy took her aside during worship and told her that she had demons living in her, and that they needed to be cast out. When he said this, she felt something try to cut off her breathing. Randy ordered that spirit to loose her and never to bother her in that way again. Everyone agreed that the following week the demons would be cast out. All week long the demons begged her to let them stay.

Julia went to the meeting and sat in a chair in the middle of the room. The first thing Randy did was to command the demons that they were not to act out nor to try any demonstrations. He ordered them to come out but they begged to stay. Randy ordered them again and one finally gave up and left. Fear...was gone. Randy asked God to not leave that area empty but to fill it with His glory. Over several meetings eight demons left, but one remained and would not leave. He played possum. No one but

Julia knew that he was there. He tried to get her to do terrible things such as to swerve into oncoming traffic or to spit in people's faces.

One evening during worship, a strong-looking angel, who looked as if he had been working out, walked up to Julia and just stood there, not uttering a sound. He never even raised a finger, but the possum demon left. It felt as if someone was pulling a sticky bandage off her insides. Moments later it was gone as God's glory rushed in to take its place. She was finally free; it was truly gone. She asked God who that angel was and He said, "That was Michael the archangel. Be free, my daughter. Now I will make you my instrument just as you have been asking me to."

Finally Julia could read the Bible and comprehend it. She thought God could now start using her but did not realize that God had just begun the healing process. The first thing He did was to give Julia a scripture, Ezekiel 11:19: "I will remove from them their heart of stone and give them a heart of flesh." She wondered what that would entail. She knew that she had a very hard heart and that there was nothing that could be done about it.

The following meeting, Randy prayed the very same scripture over her and nothing happened, but the next day Julia learned that God had a sense of humor. While standing in the dairy section of a grocery store, God healed her heart. Suddenly feeling love flood her, she burst into tears and started sobbing out loud. People gathered around to see what was wrong. Julia replied, "I'm so happy! I can feel love again."

Next, God began bringing up the painful memories that were buried so deeply within her. Julia was in so much emotional pain that she became inconsolable, even belligerent. Certain that they were hidden where neither she nor God would ever find them, each time one would come up Julia pushed it down again. One day she had had enough. They had to go.

At the next meeting she was in so much pain that everyone in the room felt it. Randy and others quickly gathered around and prayed. Randy smiled and asked Julia if she believed that Jesus had taken her place on the cross. She readily replied, "Of course I do."

"Well, then," Randy told her, "Why don't you put Jesus in your place in your memories?"

Julia had never even thought of that. The next day, one very painful memory surfaced. Julia prayed and asked Jesus to take her place in that memory. As the event began, suddenly Jesus appeared, gently pushed her out of the way and took the beating. She continued to run memories through her mind; they became mute, and the pain was gone. No longer was it her being punished, but Jesus. As memories came up, Julia continued to put Jesus in her place until there was no more pain. The memories were still there, but like watching television without sound, they could not hurt her any more, nor could the enemy torment her with them.

She prayed for those who had sexually abused her, and strangely felt love for them. But she struggled to love her father and did not miss him. Randy, when he heard this, told her that she had to honor him. Julia swore at him, something she had not done in years.

"That proves you are still upset with him," Randy insisted.

Wanting to be free of the sin of unforgiveness, Julia went home, found somewhere quiet, and asked God to help her to be completely free. After a short silence, God lovingly spoke to her. "Would you like for Me to show you why your father was the way he was?"

"Yes, God, I would," Julia answered.

All of a sudden, she saw him as a boy, weights on his shoulders, standing by a grave with his mother and siblings.

Next, she saw him standing by a different grave, but this time only him and his siblings. Now the weights were bigger and heavier. Julia felt compassion fill her heart as the pictures continued. By this time Julia was in tears. She had not known much about his childhood. He never spoke about it. He had never even told her mother. Julia realized that his pain had been greater than hers. She broke down and repented to God for not knowing her father. As the tears fell, a big change happened in her heart. She suddenly felt deep love for him and missed him. She remembered all the good things about him. The pain had been so deep that it had blocked out all the good memories: the laugh he had, his blue eyes and his handsome nose. She had always thought he had a handsome nose.

31
The Love of God

The bad memories were gone. Free to love just as deeply and as much as she wanted, even her complexion became smooth; she never again needed to wear base under her makeup. Julia was now a happy person and a better wife and friend. The only thing she missed was sitting on her father's knee and hugging his neck. She never got to do that. She loved to worship God and express her appreciation and love for Him.

One evening as she stood in the middle of the sanctuary worshiping to the music, eyes closed, she heard a voice tell her to open her eyes. She did but did not know where she was. She was facing a huge door. The room was dark. A voice told her to turn around. She did and saw a dazzlingly bright man sitting on a throne. She felt so completely loved by Him. She just stood and stared. She would have been perfectly happy just to spend all eternity gazing at Him.

His face was a mix of diamonds and gold dust. His hair was shoulder length and wavy. Every strand was a diamond. His eyes were the most welcoming blue. He was beyond beautiful. He leaned toward her and held His arms out to her and told her to come to Him.

Julia took slow timid steps toward Him. He was God. Why was she not dead? To look into God's face meant death! When she got close enough, He picked her up and set her on His lap. Getting over her timidity, she told Him she had figured out that He was God, and started kissing His cheek over and over. She leaned into Him, hugged His neck and repeatedly told Him, "You are my God."

He chuckled, pushed her back far enough so she could look into His eyes and told her, "I am also your Father." As He spoke, the chains that hung on her heart disappeared. She had sat on her Father's lap and hugged His neck. She laid her head on His chest and He held her and rocked her.

"Look into My eyes again," He told her.

She leaned back to do that. She looked into His eyes and saw so much love that she could not describe it. Nothing she could do would ever separate her from that love. At last she understood why people could die from looking into His face. His love is so strong that the human body cannot take it and live.

He set her down on the floor.

She realized that there was no light source in the room. What light was He reflecting? His hair and face radiated brilliant light. He told her that the light was in Him and was shining out of Him. She had to go, but she was to remember He was always with her.

Suddenly back in the sanctuary with the music playing, she worshiped Him more than ever.

Something changed in Julia. Compelled to tell everyone about God's love, she was limited by human language. Deciding instead to show people, she would walk up to complete strangers and hug them. She prayed for everyone who would let her, and she led many people to salvation. The enemy had a problem with that, so he stirred up people who began pointing out all the things wrong with her. She was fat, talked too much, laughed too much and too loud, and on and on. Julia shrank back a little just so she could be left alone, but her love for God never changed.

One day during worship, she again found herself in front of God's door, but this time on the outside. She banged on it and hollered to be let in. The door opened, and she stood in the doorway and looked around.

This time the light was perfect. The floor was a solid blue sapphire; the walls were opal and so were all the thrones, twelve off to the right, twelve to the left, and two straight ahead, side by side. God sat in one and Jesus in the other. Jesus was veiled; Julia was sad that He was hiding His face from her.

She wore shoes, and she thought the floor would be cold to her bare feet. But as she stepped onto it, it felt perfect, even giving in to her feet each time she took a step. Slowly she walked past the thrones. Somehow she knew that those seated on the thrones on her right were the sons of Jacob. She looked to see which one was Joseph, but they were all handsome. To her left sat the twelve apostles, all of whom waved to her as she walked.

She knew her Father and was so glad to see Him again. He welcomed her and asked her to come closer. When she did, He handed her a crown, which she took and examined. The foundation was about half an inch of gold. Set around the base were large golf ball-sized gems of various colors, including some of colors she had never seen. Above that were four-inch high sapphires about the diameter of marbles. Larger gems—almost as big as those at the base—with little peaks topped it off. It was beautiful.

"Try it on," God told her.

She hesitated. "It looks so big! It might break my neck."

"Try it on," God insisted.

So she placed it on her head. It did not weigh even an ounce. This puzzled her. God chuckled and told her, "There are no burdens in heaven."

Then He pulled out a lovely gown. The hem had all sorts of gems set into it; so did the sleeves. The whole gown shone like a beautiful summer day with a gentle breeze and everything just perfect.

"Try it on," God insisted again.

She put it on, and it was perfect. She had to ask, "Whose are these?"

"These are yours," He answered.

"Well, can I take them with me when I leave?"

"No, my precious. I'm not finished with them yet. Each time anyone mocks you for your love for Me, or even thinks unkind thoughts about you, I put more gems into your crown and gown. Now come closer; I want to show you something."

As she drew closer, she saw many jars with lids on them. He lifted the lid from one, and she felt a sorrow.

"What is that?" she asked.

"These are all your tears. I have saved everyone."

Julia was touched. She gently took off her crown and gave it back to Him, then her gown.

Her focus turned to Jesus. "Jesus, why are You hiding your face from me? I have seen You before. You were not veiled then."

"When you saw me before, you saw Me as a warrior. Now I'm here as your bridegroom."

"I must see Your face, Jesus. I must—I must—I love you. Please don't hide from me—I must see you." Julia insisted.

The veil moved off to one side, and He sat there smiling at Julia. She could see that He was so deeply in love with her. This was a very human Jewish-looking man with brown hair. His brown eyes were bright, and His face was so full of love that it glowed.

Julia could not breathe. The love was so strong it took her breath away. Now she understood what was meant by "His love held Him there." She fell on her face and started to worship Them. The twelve apostles and twelve sons of Jacob joined her in proclaiming Their goodness, love, grace and Their sacrifice for them and the whole earth. When everyone fell silent, Jesus stood and told Julia that He had something to show her. He took her hand. She did not remember walking, but now they stood by a river.

"This is the river of life," Jesus told her.

She was so amazed. She had always wanted to see it. The river seemed glad to have her there as she stood and watched. As it flowed past, its sound was like that of a harp.

Jesus took both of Julia's hands into His and told her to pay no attention to mockers. They did not know what they were doing. He said to hold on to Him whenever anyone hurt her. The enemy would try to cause her to start storing up sad memories, so they could hurt her again. She had not learned to share her heart as a child, but now she was to pile all her burdens on Him. She was weak, but He is strong. When He spoke those words, she was back from her trip.

Ever since that day an angel gives her foot rubs, mostly after she goes to bed and settles in. Sometimes she will wake up and he will be holding her hand.

She herself had been pulled from the ashes and some day, so will her whole family, just as God promises in Psalms 113:7.

Anya died at the age of ninety-eight; she too received salvation. Julia learned something from her integrity. When she got to America, someone told her she qualified for Social Security assistance. She told them loud and clear, "I did not put one penny in; I will not take one penny out. My children will take care of me, because I took care of them."

Julia learned from God that no one is broken beyond restoration and to never doubt God and His ability. He is limitless. The only limits that we have are in our carnal minds.

Amen!

November, 2009

I suffered much from the enemy, Satan, and from my father, who was ruled by Satan. My mother also suffered through unspeakable situations, but her defense was forgiveness for those who hurt her.

It was easy to see that when my mother forgave, no weapon hurled at her prospered. My mother did hurt and weep a lot, but her love and reverence for God never flickered or dimmed. She never ceased to trust Him.

I prospered spiritually from this; I know now that once the enemy plants a seed of unforgiveness and it takes root, he can fertilize it with anything: hate, jealousy, greed, even murder. I have learned that forgiveness is the best revenge. It breaks the enemy's hold on me.

Julie Cherepanov Lewin

For more information or to order <u>Pulled from the Ashes</u>, contact:

Julie Lewin

<u>http://www.pulledfromtheashes.com</u>

Breinigsville, PA USA
27 August 2010
244380BV00001B/33/P